N20

FOOD FOR T. ...

BLESSINGS

Mark Rofell

OMG EMAILS FROM TOM

MALCOLM ROTHWELL

authorHOUSE®

AuthorHouse™ UK
1663 Liberty Drive
Bloomington, IN 47403 USA
www.authorhouse.co.uk
Phone: UK TFN: 0800 0148641 (Toll Free inside the UK)
UK Local: 02036 956322 (+44 20 3695 6322 from outside the UK)

Published by AuthorHouse 07/13/2021

ISBN: 978-1-6655-9087-7 (sc)
ISBN: 978-1-6655-9086-0 (e)

This book is dedicated to the
parents of my grandchildren.

Louise and Victor; Larry and Lisa;
Oliver and Rachel; Mandie and Matthew;
Phil and Lou.

Contents

Acknowledgements

My friend and colleague the Revd. Max Millett very kindly read my first draft and made some valuable suggestions. In the beginning I wrote short chapters for grandchildren. Max pointed out that the writing was more applicable to parents than to their children. My thanks also go to my friend Dr. Carol Fry who, after I had done much cutting, editing and rewriting suggested I write short emails. She also suggested the title and persuaded me to write about the Trinity. I owe a huge debt of thanks to a colleague, Dr. Pauline Foo, and to a life-long friend, Dr. David Scarisbrick. Pauline and David gave countless suggestions and very helpful advice. They both pushed me to the limits of trying to say in simple terms what I actually do believe. The process was daunting. I really appreciate their hard work. A million thanks to them. David also, very generously, proof read the final version. My gratitude also goes to a friend and former colleague, Dr. Leslie Griffiths, for writing the foreward. Words are not enough to express my thanks. I am indebted to my daughter, Louise, for proof reading the printed version. Finally, thanks go to my wife for all her kindness, encouragement and patience.

Foreword

Malcolm Rothwell and I go back a long way. We were colleagues in the West London Mission of the Methodist Church in the late 1980s. He was the university chaplain whilst I had serious responsibilities for a wide-ranging social work programme. Each of us had to translate our theological understandings into a discourse that made as much sense on the street and in the pub as it did within the hushed interior of the sanctuary. Malcolm was very gifted for doing this. This little volume reveals that, all these years later, he hasn't lost the art of conveying spiritual or theological (or even ecclesiastical) tenets in readily accessible language. The clarity with which he writes is not achieved at the expense of rigorous thought. His learning is profound. Yet he refuses to wear it on his sleeve. It is an enviable gift.

It was a 30-day silent retreat that re-energised Malcolm for the work of apologetics. He gives a good account of it in the pages which follow. He learned to be still in the presence of the Lord, to listen for that presence, to find God in the experience of waiting. Ever since, he has spoken out of the depths he plumbed on that retreat. It's an episode that I find very compelling. But no more so than another experience he shared one Sunday evening all those years ago. With his Anglican colleague, he'd attended a conference on the subject of "clowning." He astonished us all by appearing before us dressed like "Coco the Clown," with his flapper shoes, his painted smile and his tasselled hat, - the lot. He wanted to talk about identity, appearance and reality, the hidden self. It was a brilliant example of what John Wesley called "practical divinity."

He has invested the pages that follow with large doses of his wit and charm. He does so through an epistolary exchange that touches on the core elements of the Christian faith, a kind of extended Apostles' Creed, that lays bare the length and the breadth, the height and the depth, of the love of God as expressed in Jesus. We are to suppose that his interlocutor is a former student, a young man named Tom, who is now married with a child, an engineer, someone wanting to think his way back into a faith he once had and may since have lost.

Malcolm pursues this exchange with great humility, admitting where the material he's discussing has confounded him. He appeals constantly to Tom's own lived experience. Only occasionally does his guard drop so that I felt he was more the "teacher" than the "mentor." But the discussions are rich in allusion, image and story. One homely explanation follows another – all without a patronising note. In this way the reader (as well as Tom) is helped to look at the relation between science and faith, the character of the bible and ways of approaching its truths, the work and the passion of Jesus, theories of the atonement, the importance (and ultimate incomprehensibility) of the Resurrection, patterns of prayer, the nature of the Church, and also the imperatives of ecumenism – both between different Christian traditions and between Christianity and other faiths. It was very brave of him to attempt to explain the Trinity (wandering off at times into the exotic heights of Latin and Greek phraseology).

This is a lovely handbook, a vade mecum, a useful tool, a simple guide. But let my final word suggest what to me is its greatest strength. As Malcolm and Tom engaged in the back-and-forth of their discussion, as Tom questioned some of Malcolm's replies, I found myself now and again siding with Tom. "Malcolm," I wanted to shout, "Tom's got a point there. Go back and address it." In other word, the dialectic of this book drew me in. I couldn't remain passive. I wanted to situate myself in the discussion being presented. It grabbed me.

Here's an intriguing exposition of the Christian faith, one that seeks to speak the language of our day and explore its claims honestly and relevantly and, rare in public life right now, with great humility.

Leslie Griffiths,
Former President of the Methodist Conference
and member of the House of Lords.

Introduction

Let's be honest, membership of the Christian Church in the West is declining. There are many reasons for this; one of them is that belief in God as a supernatural being is on the wane. A major contributory factor to this decline happened during the Great War when realisation dawned that God was not going to save soldiers from the horrors of the trenches and end the war by Christmas 1914. During World War II God did not intervene and prevent six million Jews from being exterminated in horrendous death camps. Viewpoints surrounding the existence of a supernatural God have also been greatly influenced by major advances in science. For example, in our hospitals we now have scanners, keyhole surgery, organ transplants, chemotherapy, and fertility treatments. We may choose to pray for healing, but would be unwise not to consult a GP and use up to date diagnostics and recommended treatments.

Not only has our view of God changed but there is considerable doubt as to our understanding of traditional Christian beliefs. I have heard it said that these are no more than gobbledegook. For many, making sense of the Christian faith in today's secular world has become impossible and they have left the church and discarded Christianity. The baby has gone out with the bath water.

This book represents an honest attempt to investigate and to understand what God might still mean for us today. I believe wholeheartedly that the Christian faith is not locked in the pages of the bible, in the Nicene Creed, in the sermons of John Wesley the hymns of his brother Charles or, indeed, in the sermons of the American evangelist Billy Graham. We have to try and make sense of the concept of God, the life and death of Jesus and the bible. For some this may feel like a betrayal of traditional ways of understanding God, but for others I hope it will bring enlightenment, liberation and a zest for living.

These emails are written to a friend of mine called Thomas, otherwise known as Tom. He is raising a whole series of questions which I am attempting to answer. I met Tom just over twenty years ago when he was a university student and I was a chaplain. He didn't attend chaplaincy events and so our paths didn't cross very much until he found himself without a roof over his head. We were able to accommodate him at the manse for a few months while he sorted out something more permanent.

For a long time he has struggled with his Christian faith largely because he assumes that to be a Christian you have to believe in Adam and Eve, the Virgin Birth and everything in the bible without question. He has become disillusioned and finds himself beginning to have major doubts about his faith. This is a fairly common phenomenon. I have often come across people of my generation who say they used to go to Sunday school and their granddad was either a Methodist Minister or a Lay Preacher. They themselves no longer attend a church, neither do their children. There are multiple reasons for this but I think one reason, as I have said, is the difficulty of making sense of the Christian faith in the world in which we now live.

I really hope you enjoy the journey through these emails. It seems to me that we have to keep on asking questions even if the answers are not always clear. The ideal is to ask your own questions and keep looking for the answers that satisfy your journey through life. We are all on a journey and part of that journey is learning to ponder the questions. Quite by accident I came across this quote on google by Rainer Maria Rilke which I think is very appropriate.

"Be patient toward all that is unsolved in your heart and try to love the questions themselves, like locked rooms and like books that are now written in a very foreign tongue. Do not now seek the answers, which cannot be given you because you would not be able to live them. And the point is, to live everything. Live the questions now. Perhaps you will then gradually, without noticing it, live along some distant day into the answer."

LABELS

Dear Malcolm,

I wonder whether you remember me. I was one of your Methodist students when you were the university chaplain about twenty years ago. In those days, I always seemed to disagree with you because, of course, I had all the answers and I was always right. How things have changed. You seemed to be so radical and I was a very conservative evangelical. I hope you don't mind me writing to you but I am confident that you can sort me out. However, before we get on to questions of faith can you tell me whether your beliefs have changed and how you describe yourself theologically.

Dear Tom,

It's really good to hear from you, a blast from the past. I am more than happy to try and 'sort you out' as long as you don't think I have all the answers. Of course, I remember you. We had many a long discussion but nothing I said seemed to make any difference. That isn't surprising. People cannot be argued into the Kingdom of God any more than they can be persuaded into falling in love. As St. Paul writes to the Corinthians, 'Where is the debater of this age? Has not God made foolish the wisdom of the world?..........for God's foolishness is wiser than human wisdom'. It is all there in chapter one.

You asked about my beliefs. I confess I have never been a conservative evangelical.

Those who hold such views tend to be quite dogmatic about God and I feel very uncomfortable when people assume they know all there is to know about God. They are absolutely certain of their faith and God is somehow domesticated and finds a home in their back pocket. Everything is cut and dried. Oh that it were! God remains a mystery to be explored. The life of faith is a never ending voyage of discovery.

Conservative evangelicals tend to hold a very literal view of the bible. They argue that the bible is the supreme authority. It is literally the inspired word of God. However, I think today we have a different understanding of God to when the bible was written. The contents actually cover a period from about 1500 B.C.E to about 100 A.D. Not only do we see the physical world differently but culturally we are in a different place. For example, the bible takes it for granted that some people will be slaves. That is most definitely not the Christian view point today. Furthermore if one says that the bible is the supreme authority, where does that leave tradition, human reason, scientific discovery, or, indeed, our own experience?

However, you can certainly call me evangelical. I want other people to have a sense of the love and forgiveness of God and the powerful attraction of Jesus in a world where there is so much human suffering. Some people say that Christians use Jesus as a crutch to support them but for me Jesus is an inspiration. The world would be a far better place if people were motivated by love rather than power and hate. You won't be aware of the fact, but some years ago I went on a thirty day silent retreat. That, for me was a very profound experience of the presence of God.

Conservative evangelicals tend to point to a specific time in their life when they were 'born again' or 'saved'. For me, and for many others, growing in faith is a much more gradual process. That retreat profoundly deepened my faith in God. You see the Christian life is a journey. There may be moments of greater clarity, and sometimes moments of total disillusionment, but God accompanies us each step of the way. We don't, as it were, arrive when we are saved, or when we are baptised. In one sense, we never arrive, 'for now we see in a mirror dimly, but then we shall see face to face' as St. Paul wrote to the Corinthians. God is our destination.

I suppose you could describe me as a liberal evangelical. But that is an insufficient pigeon hole because I want to add the words radical and traditional.

I am traditional because I am still a Methodist minister. My belief in the importance of the church is paramount although I do have severe reservations about the church as an institution. Sometimes it has got things horribly wrong. For example, it took a long time in most denominations before women were accepted as preachers and ministers. The Roman Catholic Church still doesn't allow women priests and sadly, there has been the scandal of sexual abuse. I use the word radical, as opposed to revolutionary, because a radical works from the inside and tries to get to the root of problems. Any change comes by working from the inside and not by working on the outside along a revolutionary path of destruction.

To come back to your questions you could describe me as a traditional, radical, liberal evangelical. How about that for confusing labels? My beliefs have changed a little but, over the years, my faith has deepened.

Lots of love, Malcolm

DOUBTING THOMAS

Since my university days when you were my chaplain, I have become very disillusioned with the church and developed serious doubts about my former Christian beliefs. I used to be absolutely certain about my close relationship with God. As a student I interpreted all events on campus and at home in a very black and white way. I have become very disheartened by my lack of certainty in the Christian faith, in fact, in the real world of work I find it all very unsettling.

I hope you don't mind me troubling you in this way.

Dear Tom, as I said before, don't expect me to have all the answers. Sometimes it is more important to ask the questions even if the answers aren't forth coming. I get very worried with people who stubbornly refuse to explore the relevance of the Christian faith in the twenty first century. People go to church and are often expected to leave their minds and brains in blinkers on the doorstep. Yet Jesus instructs us to believe not only with our hearts but also with our minds.

You seem to be living up to your names sake – Doubting Thomas! Let me assure you that there is nothing wrong with having doubts. I remember reading a book years ago called The Christian Agnostic. That seems to me to be a reasonable position to adopt. There are many things in the Christian faith that we can't be certain about. The existence of God and precisely what happened at the first Easter are two obvious examples. That is precisely where faith comes in. Those who are longing for certainty are longing for something that is less than faith. The New Testament doesn't offer certainty but it does offer love, forgiveness, grace, and above all, faith. We are brought to the point of accepting God's love, even in our turbulent world, through faith, not through certainty.

As an engineer you are used to dealing with facts but you know as well as I do that there is something called Heisenberg's uncertainty principle. We cannot measure simultaneously and accurately both the position and movement of even a single molecule. The mathematics involved is complicated, and the principle typically relates to microscopic particles. It implies that certainty and uncertainty at the molecular level are still being questioned by physicists and molecular biologists. Surely, then, it is not unreasonable that Christians can discuss their faith in the modern world in terms of questions that cannot be resolved by simple one word answers.

In many cases, science deals with probabilities and

works on the basis of a given hypothesis. I know someone once said I have no need of the God hypothesis, but it is a concept that works for me. Just as scientists use a battery of experimental processes to prove or disprove their hypotheses, so, in the same way, Christians can test their hypothesis that God exists by examining the evidence.

There are a number of facts which help to support the hypothesis the prime one being that a person called Jesus actually lived and was crucified. There is more historical evidence for this than for the life of Julius Caesar. It is quite amazing that even two thousand years after his death, Jesus still has the power to transform lives. Furthermore there is plenty of historical evidence that the Christian faith has produced artwork, music, poetry, beautiful architecture and many other things which still benefit millions of people.

I also find the story of the early church very inspiring. Individuals were prepared to die for their faith rather than say 'Caesar is Lord'. These people were frightened. They lived in an occupied country and were often persecuted and tortured. What was it that made them so strong in their faith? Had they actually seen Jesus? Did they have an experience of his power? What was it that drew people to Jesus in the first place? Ordinary people, fishermen, farmers, carpenters, gave up their work, their security, their livelihood, and followed him. Even some women gave up their daily lives and followed him. That, in itself, is quite extraordinary. Even more so is the fact that the crucifixion didn't mark the end of what

Jesus had started. It proved to be the beginning. The first disciples had some kind of powerful experience which enabled them to teach and preach in the face of enormous opposition.

The story of St. Paul is also very exciting. When you view his experience on the Damascus Road it is fair to say that something dramatic happened. Instead of persecuting Christians he became one of them. Not only that, as you well know, Paul journeyed throughout the known world preaching the Good News. His letters alone bear testimony to that fact.

I know that someone once said that I have no need of the God hypothesis but it is a concept that works for me.

So you see Tom, faith is not a leap in the dark. Faith is based on some things that we know for certain. I could also include my own experience of God whilst on a retreat. Maybe I will mention that at a later stage but it is very important not to disregard one's personal experience. That is one of the ways in which God speaks to us. I wonder what your experience of God has been. You seem to be discounting your earlier experiences as though they don't matter.

Obviously I am getting a bit long in the tooth now and you will see things differently. As someone once said, we don't see things as they are, we see things as we are. I wonder how you are.

Please feel free to write again.
Love and blessings, Malcolm.

p.s. a friend of mine pointed me in the direction of this poem by Malcolm Guite. I thought you might like it.

St. Thomas the Apostle.

"We do not know... how can we know the way?"
Courageous master of the awkward question,
You spoke the words the others dared not say
And cut through their evasion and abstraction.
Oh doubting Thomas, father of my faith,
You put your finger on the nub of things
We cannot love some disembodied wraith,
But flesh and blood must be our king of kings.
Your teaching is to touch, embrace, anoint,
Feel after Him and find Him in the flesh.
Because He loved your awkward counter-point
The Word has heard and granted you your wish.
Oh place my hands with yours, help me divine
The wounded God whose wounds are healing mine.

IS THERE A GOD?

Dear Malcolm,

Many thanks for your reply. We'll come on to the life of Jesus later. For the moment I want to talk about God.

From his studies on the origin of the solar system, the brilliant French mathematician and astronomer Pierre LaPlace concluded he had no need of the God hypothesis. You see, many people have eschewed religion with God as a prop, and have come to believe in themselves, a faith in their own ability. I now believe it is better to stand on my own two feet than wait for God's miracles. The concept of a God has become just one of my stumbling blocks.

You see I have been brought up in the space age. The universe is huge beyond imagination and you know the story of the Russian astronaut who said "now I know there isn't a God because I've not seen one whilst I've been in space". What do you make of that?

Hi Tom, an interesting question. Space travel and going to the moon were distant dreams when I was young. Now it is almost common place. Apparently, there are lots of satellites orbiting round the earth watching our every move. I don't understand how they work but, apparently satnavs and spy networks are dependent on them.

Our solar system seems to be a very orderly place and astronomers happily talk about lots of planets or stars being light years away. You know what a light year is but I had to look it up on Google. It is way beyond my imagination to think in terms of a beam of light travelling a distance of six trillion miles in one year – a light year. Imagine that! Google also tells me that our nearest star, Alpha Centauri, is 4.4 light years away. I can't get my head around that. We don't actually know whether the universe is finite or whether it goes off into infinity.

This all has a huge impact on how we have traditionally understood God. We know that in biblical times, people explained the world as being built in three storeys. The storey up above was called heaven and the storey below was called hell. Humans lived on the earth in the storey in between heaven and hell. The sky was thought to be a kind of lid which had lights in it –the sun, moon and stars. Naturally, God lived in heaven and from there God could observe all that was going on down below. People thought that God rewarded those who were living good lives, and punished those who weren't so good.

The bible speaks about God sending his son 'down' into the world and talks of Jesus 'ascending' back up to heaven. Many of our hymns still use this same imagery of 'up' and 'down'. Common parlance talks about God being 'him upstairs' as people point their finger skywards. Historically, God has a white beard, and observes his creation sitting on a throne; Father Christmas to a tee.

Clearly, with research providing a broader understanding of the universe, we can no longer think like that. I certainly don't think of God in that kind of way. God isn't 'up there' ready to intervene at a moment's notice, ready to grant us our wish list, or even to intervene in world affairs and change the order of things. The idea of a god as a heavenly supernatural being who waves a magic wand at our behest has to go. It is very tempting to believe that God acts like that but it can be very misleading and, I think, takes people into atheism. "If God is supposed to be almighty, then I don't like what God is doing with the world. Why doesn't he do something about the wars in the Middle East and assist thousands of refugees living in tents." I'm sure you have heard people argue along these lines and they come to the conclusion that a loving God does not exist.

I had something of an epiphany when I was a student in the sixties. I went along to a Sunday Service where Sydney Carter was preaching. You may not have heard of him but Carter wrote 'Lord of the Dance' and

'When I needed a neighbour'. The Vietnam War had been waging all through the decade and I had heard many preachers earnestly praying that God would bring an end to the conflict. Carter posed a question to the congregation. How many of us could point to Vietnam on a map? This drew no response.

How could members of the congregation expect God to intervene and sort things out when they didn't even know the geographical position of Vietnam? This is a picture of God that has him (whether God is male is a debatable issue) on top of the pantheon of Gods. This is God Almighty but in actual fact the New Testament paints a picture of a vulnerable God. God puts himself into our hands in the form of a baby. This is what we celebrate every Christmas. Jesus, who Christians believe is the Son of God, was born. Babies are very vulnerable. The first chapter of Corinthians talks about the 'weakness' of God. This is not to do with physical strength but refers to the crucifixion of Jesus which, on the face of it, appears to be very weak. This historical event is at the heart of Christianity. There is no sense of control, coercion or manipulation in that cross, only vulnerability.

A recurring metaphor for Jesus in the New Testament is as the Lamb of God. In the Old Testament a spotless lamb was sacrificed by the High Priest to atone for the peoples' sins. In the New Testament this idea is carried through and Jesus is pictured as the unblemished Lamb of God who is sacrificed so that sins are forgiven. I am sure we shall come on to this at a later stage of your inquiries but, for now, let me say that this is only one interpretation of the death of Jesus. However, undoubtedly, the metaphor portrays Jesus as something very vulnerable, a lamb.

Maybe we have to dispense with the word 'God' altogether because the word is filled with all sorts of associations from the past. But what do we replace it with? Of course, God is not a thing or a person that we could compare to other things or people. I have heard God described as 'essence' whereas we humans are 'existence'. Some describe God as 'absolute love', the kind that we see in the life of Jesus. Others say that God is the 'ground of our being', deep inside each one of us. These definitions help, but only up to a point. A definition which I personally like is as follows;

'God is not an old man outside the earth living in the sky, but rather a creative energy that is in and through the whole earth. This creative energy isn't a human being – male or female – rather it is within and underlying all beings (and animals and plants) earth, air, and water. It is personal and transpersonal; it is the energy of renewal and transformation that was the basis of all creation. This is the divinity that I had experienced every day. This is the god to which I could relate, had been relating, and could continue to relate in my daily live'.

I think this is by Barbara Brown Taylor but I'm not sure where I saw it!!

Let's face it, the whole concept of God is very elusive and if we could define God exactly, then he/

she wouldn't be God. As I have said before the only way we can talk of God is through metaphor. God is the 'light' which lights us all up when we are born and God is the one who gives us life. Yes, I know, lots of people ignore that light but that's another story. If we want to get in touch with this God then we need to become vulnerable ourselves. In other words, we have to ask. This is difficult because we live in a world that extols the 'self –made man or woman'. We applaud status, possessions, cars, money, holidays etc. These are things we can achieve. We can't 'achieve' God by our own efforts. Only by swallowing our pride and asking can God come in. My experience is that God does not play hard to get. Do you remember the parable of the prodigal son? The father is waiting for his son to come back home.

Of course, it was also thought in biblical times that God was male. Although there are some female biblical images of God that are often overlooked, the predominant view was that God was male. This is not surprising because the culture was very patriarchal. Today, many people still think of God as male and this is deeply embedded in our culture. I wonder, though, what it actually means. I don't wish to embarrass you but does it mean that God shaves or that God has male sexual organs? I prefer to think of God as having no gender or, to put it another way, God is male and female. Actually, the book of Genesis does say that we are all made in God's image, both male and female.

I hope this helps in your thinking about God. Maybe

it confuses you! I very much like something called Pascal's wager. "One cannot come to the knowledge of God's existence through reason alone, so the wise thing to do is to live your life as if God does exist because such a life has everything to gain and nothing to lose. If we live as though God exists, and God does indeed exist, we have gained heaven. If He doesn't exist, we have lost nothing".

Just a thought about satnavs before I finish. The woman who speaks, at least it's a woman who speaks to me, always knows where I am! She knows the name of the road and not only that, she knows if I take a wrong turn and tells me what to do about it. Furthermore, if they are switched on, she knows just where everybody else is. EVERYBODY else. You see, Tom, I grew up in a very simple world and I just find things like this absolutely amazing. To come back to your question about God, maybe it helps to think that God is like a satnav!! All you have to do is switch on and listen – and the listening is prayer. Perhaps you will want to talk about prayer at a later stage.

Lots of love, Malcolm.

p.s. God is like exploring a mystery. Nothing else in religion is quite so important.

WHAT ABOUT THE BIBLE?

Hi Malcolm, I will certainly want to raise the issue of prayer but for the moment I have been thinking about what you said about God. It is very challenging, what you say makes sense, after leaving university I found it impossible to believe that God lived somewhere in the bright blue sky. I was brought up to read the bible and to think of it as the inspired word of God. If we start saying some of it isn't true then it is a short step to say that none of it is true. In fact, some people do say that the bible is a complete work of fiction.

Hi Tom, many people think that everything in the bible is absolutely true. What is not recognised is that the bible is not just one book although it looks just like one! You know that but, like many people, you have not thought through the implications. The fact is that the bible actually contains sixty-six different books written by many different authors and written over hundreds of years. This means that there are different kinds of writing in the bible – history, poetry, prophecy, letters, hymns and so on. Did all the different authors conspire to write fiction? Surely that is stretching the imagination a bit too far.

Some people hold the view that the bible is absolutely true, but this raises the question of what we mean by 'true'. There are different kinds of truth. For example, if I said I had a frog in my throat, or butterflies in my tummy, or a chip on my shoulder you wouldn't think that these things were literally true. Yet, they could be true, in some sense. They are a metaphorical way of speaking. Some writings do not have to be literally true for them to be meaningful and completely truthful. Forgive me for being very simplistic.

When the bible talks about Jesus ascending into heaven and sitting at the right hand of God, that is a metaphor. It does not imply he is God's right hand man, this could be interpreted as handy man, a DIY expert. The meaning is simply that Christ is uniquely special to God and has his authority. To sit at the right hand of an earthly king was a place of honour, denoting special trust, authority from, and relationship with the king. This was something that was understood without needing explanation at the time. Sitting at the right hand of the king meant that you acted with his authority. Those who came to you would treat you with respect and obedience, as if you were the king yourself. This is one of the many demonstrations in the bible, that is not readily understood by us in our time but made perfect sense to the culture as it was then.

Of course, God doesn't actually have hands. The only hands God has are ours. There's something for you to think about! I am reminded of the old joke about the boy who came home from school and said that God was very clever because he had created the world with one hand. When his mother asked why the lad replied, 'because Jesus was sitting on his right hand'. Apologies for that Tom.

When we say that Jesus is the bread of life or the light of the world, we don't mean that Jesus is a sliced loaf or a candle. These are also metaphorical ways of speaking. A metaphor compares two unlike things. The bible uses metaphors extensively as a way of illustrating it's message, they are used in order to create an impact. When God is described as a rock, shepherd, a light, these descriptions paint a vivid picture in the mind of readers.

Metaphors are also widely used in everyday conversation. Perhaps your wife thinks you are the apple of her eye. This doesn't mean that she has an apple core for an eye! It means she loves you very much and you are very special to her. I'm sorry if all this sounds very obvious, but it is very important to understand that there are different kinds of truth.

As I pointed out in my last letter, our concepts of God have changed since the bible was written. This is especially the case with images given in the Old Testament. I have written about this in a previous book, but just let me give you one example. If you tend to disobey your parent, are a bit rebellious, or a drunkard, and that is surely not you, then you will come to a very sticky end. You will be taken out of the city and stoned! You can read about this in Deuteronomy 21: 18-21. Thank goodness our views have changed. I could cite many other examples but I run the risk of boring you.

The other thing to remember about the bible is that it isn't a scientific text book. It was written by people who had a belief in God, and it is written from a non- scientific perspective. Do I need to tell you this?! Our lives have been forever changed by the likes of Copernicus, Galileo, Newton, Darwin, Freud. More recently, Watson and Crick have discovered the structure of DNA and this has revolutionised genetics, medicine and police work.

Can it really be right, as the bible asserts, that man, Adam, was made from the dust of the earth, and Eve was made out of Adam's rib? Doesn't Darwin's theory of evolution suggest that we are all descended from a type of primate animal? Chimpanzees have DNA very similar to our own.

We also now know that the world is not about 4,000 years old but more like 13 billion years old. Christians cannot discount the findings of science. At one time, it was thought that the earth was the centre of the universe but then along came Galileo and Copernicus who showed that the sun is the centre, not the earth. Everything revolves round the sun. This means we now view our planet and ourselves from a completely different perspective. We are part of a very large universe and we are not the centre of it. We now take this for granted but it took the church a few hundred years to actually take this discovery on board.

Forgive me Tom for writing all this. I'm sure you know far more about these things than I ever will. However, it is important to follow through the implications of our advanced scientific understandings. Religion is constantly reacting to scientific advances, never the other way round. To put it in a nut shell, the bible is not literally true but it is a collection of books that need to be taken seriously. If you, Tom, take the bible seriously and realise the different kinds of writings and messages it contains, then it may change the way you think and act. I think that many people who discount the importance of the bible in today's society have never bothered to read it.

Let me finish with an important point. The bible can be really helpful. It continues to have a great impact on most people who take the trouble to read it. People can be touched, comforted, consoled, disturbed, inspired and uplifted by what they find in its pages. Historically, people like Martin Luther and John Wesley found it life changing to read Paul's letter to the Romans. Who has not been uplifted at a wedding service to hear the great hymn to love in 1 Corinthians 13, or been consoled at a funeral service with the words of psalm 23? I know it is obvious but if you want to learn about God, then read about the life of Jesus, as found in the New Testament. Jesus asserts (John 14:9) that anyone who has seen him has seen God. Personally, I find the words of Jesus are often very challenging. For example, he talks about loving others, even our enemies. If that isn't enough, he talks about praying for those who persecute us, going the extra mile and turning the other cheek. What a challenge that is. Who ever thought that being a Christian was a soft option! I could give lots more examples but that is enough for now! Blessings, Malcolm

p.s. A bible that's falling apart usually belongs to someone who isn't. (Charles H. Spurgeon)

WHAT ABOUT ADAM AND EVE?

Hi Malcolm, I think you have been a bit patronising to say the least. I may be confused but you assume I haven't done any thinking at all. For example, surely it is possible to believe the bible is inspired without taking it literally. Moreover, if people want to take the bible literally, can't we allow them that perspective? What do you say to people who claim the bible is the word of God? Furthermore, science certainly doesn't explain everything and you make it sound as though religion has no solid base but simply reacts to the latest scientific discovery.

You briefly mentioned Adam and Eve in your last email. I can happily go along with Darwin and his theory of evolution, but what do you make of the Genesis story? Is it just a story?

Hi Tom, many apologies for coming across as patronising. Please let me know if it happens again. I agree entirely that the bible is inspired whether you take it literally or not. If people want to take the bible literally, then that is up to them, of course. The problem for me is that it would mean believing that the world was created in six days, talking snakes, surviving in the belly of a big fish, and a whole host of other things that I find difficult to take on board.

I also agree that science doesn't explain everything. Beauty, as they say, is found in the eye of the beholder, not in a scientific experiment. God remains a mystery and is not found in a test-tube. The morality of what is right or wrong cannot be determined by scientific experiment. However, I actually do think that religion adapts to scientific discovery. A simple example would be that the earth is not the centre of the universe as was once believed but the sun is the centre around which all else revolves. There is, though, a solid base to religion. For example, I have no doubt that Jesus is a figure of history who was crucified, his mother was called Mary and this happened when Herod was king. So much is historical fact, as is the rise of the early Christian church in spite of much persecution.

For me the bible tells us how the Israelites responded to God and then, in the New Testament, how the early Christian communities responded to God. The bible tells us about people's experiences of God. If you want to read further into this I suggest an excellent book by Marcus Borg entitled 'Reading the bible again, for the first time'. I can do no better than quote Borg "rather than seeing God as scripture's ultimate author, I see the bible as the response of ......communities to their experience of God. As such, it contains their stories of God, their perceptions of God's character and will, their prayers to and praise of God….their religious and ethical practices, and their understanding of what faithfulness to God involves….the bible thus tells us about how *they* saw things, not about how *God* sees things." (p.22)

As for Adam and Eve, there are certainly some people who believe they actually existed and God created the world in six days. As you know, they are called creationists. They take a very fundamentalist view of the bible. Everything in it is literally true. I've already explained that there are different kinds of truth, for example, metaphor. Something can be true without being literally true. There is another kind of writing in the bible and that is parable.

Let's take, for example, the parable of the Good Samaritan. A man was out walking in the country and thieves set upon him. Two people, a priest and a Levite, saw him lying there and didn't take any notice. They carried on walking. Then along came a Samaritan who helped the man and took him to the nearest inn where he stayed for the night. I'm sure many people believe that this event didn't literally happen, although it may have done. The whole point of the parable is its meaning. The man who was robbed was helped by a Samaritan, who was thought to be an enemy. You remember the priest and the Levite walked by on the other side. They thought the man was dead and was therefore, for them, untouchable. The message of this parable is that we have to be a good neighbour to anyone who needs our help, and not ignore them and walk by on the other side.

I find it helpful to categorise the stories of Adam and Eve and the creation as parables. If you read the first creation story in the first chapter of Genesis you will notice that on the first three days God created, day and night, sky and ocean, land and vegetation. On the fourth day God created the sun, moon and stars. You don't have to be a scientist to realise this order of creation poses problems, this difficulty has been recognised for hundreds of years. The story doesn't conflict with modern science because it has many interpretations. Basically, the story is saying all that has been created comes from God. The story is an affirmation of the goodness of creation. Yes, I know, people have spoiled it and continue to do so; this brings us to the second creation story.

This creation account is in the second chapter of Genesis and is about the creation of the first man and woman, Adam and Eve. Interestingly, the name of Adam is not mentioned until the end of chapter four. He is simply referred to as the man. The word 'adam' is the Hebrew word for humankind. In other words, the story is not about one single man, it is about all of us. As you know, the story informs us that the first woman, Eve, was created out of the rib of Adam. Eve is not a name but means 'mother of all living'. They live in a very special place called the Garden of Eden in which there is a tree of knowledge of good and evil and a tree of life. The couple are not supposed to eat anything from these trees, but a talking serpent tempts them to do so. They succumb to the temptation and, as a result, God expels them from the Garden, from paradise. Furthermore God punishes Eve by saying 'I will greatly increase your pains in child-bearing', and punishes Adam by saying 'cursed is the ground because of you, through painful toil you will eat of it all the days of your life'. You can read about all this in Genesis chapter three. The symbolism of the names, the special trees, God 'walking' in the Garden and the talking snake all indicate this is a parable.

At one level the parable offers an explanation why child birth is so painful and difficult, why snakes crawl on the ground and the sweat and toil of hard, manual labour. At another level the story is about the desire of humankind to eat fruit from the tree of knowledge, and become like God or saying that we don't need God. The parable is also reflecting on the cause of pain and suffering in the world and suggesting that problems begin when we empower ourselves and begin to act as though we are God.

Another meaning of the parable is about an awakening of self-awareness in the human mind. You remember that Adam and Eve saw they were naked. They realised they were distinct from each other and distinct from creation. Sadly, this separation from the world around us has continued and humankind has seen itself as distinct from creation rather than part and parcel of it. Perhaps through recent scientific discoveries and environmental awareness we are beginning to realise that we are all responsible for God's creation. Moreover, there is only one planet earth, and we all need to take care of it, as well as each other.

So you see Tom, these stories can be true and meaningful without being literally true. Moreover, if interpreted in this way, they are not in conflict with scientific discoveries. Science is actually helping us to see our proper place in creation. The earth is billions of years older than the date suggested by the bible. There is an immense amount of information about the beginnings of the world coming from geology, astronomy, physics and cave paintings. Christianity does not oppose intellectual debate and constructive criticism. Christians have to use their brains. Jesus, in the first commandment, exhorts us to love God with all our hearts, souls and minds. Moreover, science seeks to answer the how questions, whereas religion seeks to answer the why questions. How does my bedroom light work? We know that the switch and wires have been connected to electricity. Why is the light shining? Because my bedroom is dark and I want to read my book.

Why is there such a diversity of life on this tiny planet in the midst of an infinite universe? Why do any of us exist at all? These are religious or philosophical questions.

Lots of love, Malcolm.

IS CHRISTMAS ONE
BIG FAIRY STORY?

Dear Malcolm, You seem to assume that you are the only one using your brain! Even if people take the bible literally, this does not mean they are not using their brains. Furthermore, not everyone has a university degree, are they therefore to be excluded from God's kingdom? I once heard a preacher saying there is a danger of killing Christianity by degrees! In any case, surely there are many questions about God that cannot be answered simply by thought alone.

I can go along with most of what you say, but then we were talking about something in the Old Testament. What about the New Testament? Let's take the Christmas stories as an example. Are these accounts of the birth of Jesus just stories as well? Are they also parables not to be taken literally?

Dear Tom, forgive me yet again. Of course you are right and so was your preacher friend. There can be a very real danger in being too intellectual. How arrogant of me to assume it is only people like me who can think. God is ready to accept everyone wherever they are on their Christian journey, and there are certainly many unanswered questions about God. I hope I have not given the impression that I know all the answers! In the final analysis we know precious little about the mystery we call God. I sincerely hope I am not endangering anyone's faith. My aim is simply to try to make the Christian faith intelligible, at least to me, and hopefully to others, hence these emails.

I just love Christmas. Some of the carols I really enjoy singing. However, for me the great thing about Christmas is not just about presents and singing carols, it is hearing those wonderful words from the gospel stories.

'In those days a decree went out from Emperor Augustus that all the world should be registered'.

'In that region there were shepherds living in the fields, keeping watch over their flock by night'.

'Now the birth of Jesus the Messiah took place in this way'.

'In the time of King Herod, after Jesus was born in Bethlehem of Judea, wise men from the East came to Jerusalem asking "Where is the child who has been born king of the Jews? For we have observed his star at its rising, and have come to pay him homage".'

Listening to these passages every year brings goose pimples on my arms. They bring a feeling of assurance and hope in a very unsettled world. However, to state the obvious, there were no reporters present at the birth of Jesus, or television crews or cameras of any description. Moreover, the birth accounts were written long after the death of Jesus. Indeed, the earliest New Testament writer, St. Paul, doesn't mention the birth of Jesus neither does Mark, the earliest gospel writer. Moreover, neither Paul nor Mark record that Jesus was born in a special way. One can only assume that the birth stories of Jesus were of no importance to Paul or Mark, or maybe it was important but they just didn't record it. Certainly Paul wasn't writing a biography of Jesus so why would he mention Jesus' birth?

As you probably know, Tom, there are two accounts of the birth of Jesus. One is in Luke's gospel where the first two quotations come from, and the second is in Matthew's gospel, where the last two quotations come from. Some people try to reconcile the two accounts but, although there are some common elements, they are quite different. Both versions cannot be historically accurate. Luke talks about shepherds and Matthew mentions visitors from the East, although we don't actually know their names and number. Matthew refers to a special star that Luke doesn't mention at all. Luke says there was no room at the inn; but, interestingly, there is no record of an inn keeper although I guess there is one in every school nativity play. Since Mary and Joseph were travelling to Bethlehem, their home town, it seems strange no family members could provide accommodation. Would it be feasible for a heavily pregnant woman to ride approximately a hundred miles from Nazareth to Bethlehem on a donkey?

In Luke's account the central character is Mary, the mother of Jesus. You will remember that an angel appears to Mary in a dream and tells her that she is going to bear a son conceived by the Holy Spirit. On the other hand, the central character in Matthew's gospel is Joseph, the father of Jesus. God appears to Joseph in five dreams and one includes the news that Mary's unexpected pregnancy is from God. Mary hardly gets a mention. You may well ask what is going on. Are these stories true or not? What actually happened? Sadly I think we shall never know. Does that matter? What really matters is what do the different stories mean? What message are the writers trying to convey?

I could go into detail about how Matthew uses Old Testament imagery, and is writing for the benefit of Jewish people. Luke is writing for the benefit of people who were not Jews, but if I include too much biblical research, I fear I will bore you to tears. Some Christians say that the stories are literally true, that things happened just as they were written. Taking the stories literally, for me, somehow makes them more like fairy stories and so the Good News about Jesus becomes a story like Cinderella. Nothing could be further from the truth, although I need to tell you that Cinderella does have a moral message. Don't be mean and horrible to someone who isn't good looking and has no money. She is just as worthy as her sisters to a handsome boyfriend and of being 'happy ever after'.

Both gospel stories are trying to communicate, in

their own way, that Jesus comes from God. To say, for example, 'Jesus was born in Bethlehem to proud parents, Mary and Joseph' is just too prosaic, too ordinary and this birth announcement tells you nothing about Jesus and who he was. Matthew and Luke used the language and story- telling technique of their day to describe it. In the light of what they had seen and heard about the life of Jesus they believed that he was the one who had a different kind of life to offer; not the Caesars or dictators of the world. Jesus is the one who will bring light into the world, and into our lives and nothing will ever put that light out. The gospel stories are strong accounts of who Jesus is. He is related to God in a very special way and that way is so special, to talk about his birth in ordinary language is just not sufficient.

I think that the doctrine of the virgin birth is one way of saying that Jesus was so special that his birth wasn't natural. The biblical evidence for this is dubious. The gospel writers drew upon the prophetic message in Isaiah. 'Therefore the Lord himself will give you a sign. Look, the young woman is with child and shall bear a son, and shall name him Immanuel'. (Is. 7:14) Note that the words 'young woman' have been used. The Hebrew word for young woman, signifies a girl of childbearing age without reference to virginity. The word has been mistranslated in New Testament Greek as 'virgin'. In any case, Isaiah is talking about his own immediate circumstances in the year 735 BC, not the distant future. It is highly unlikely that the king at the time of this prophecy, Ahaz, would have found comfort in a prophecy that would not come to pass for another eight hundred years, and yet Matthew uses it to show that the prophecy has been fulfilled in Jesus. There is a theological reason here. The intention is to show that Jesus is the fulfilment of the desires of the Jewish people and that he is the promised Messiah.

Note that Luke differs from Matthew in depicting a virginal conception rather than a virgin birth although this, of itself, does not deny a virgin birth. There is nothing in Luke that suggests Joseph did not have sexual relations with Mary after the angel visited her to say that she was going to give birth to a son, although I admit that Matthew says that the couple did not have sexual relations. Matt. 1:24 All of this does not mean that God was not involved. I am sure that God's Spirit was involved and the birth of Jesus was an act of God, but one can truly say that without having to admit that Mary was somehow mysteriously impregnated with sperm by the Holy Spirit. Incidentally, the Hebrew word for spirit is feminine.

When we have experienced a great event we want to tell others about it, and we often exaggerate to make a point. You know, Tom, that the great event the early Christian writers experienced was Easter. No doubt we shall talk again about the resurrection of Jesus but, for the moment, let me say that all the New Testament is written in the light of the resurrection experience. Matthew and Luke are no exception. They had no doubt who Jesus was, nothing less than the Son of God. Their purpose in writing a gospel is so that others might come to have faith in

Jesus. Their concern is not so much with writing a precise historical account as with preaching the Good News. A gospel is a proclamation of a living faith. The faith of the early Christians was such a reality they were willing to be whipped, stoned, imprisoned and even crucified for it.

As a final point, let me give you another example. The visitors from the East brought gifts to the infant Jesus. Have you ever thought what strange gifts they were? Gold, frankincense and myrrh are totally inappropriate for a toddler. Have you ever wondered what happened to those gifts? The implication is that Matthew is not writing an historical account but he is using these gifts to tell us the significance of Jesus. Gold represents the kingship of Jesus, frankincense a symbol of his priestly role, and myrrh prefiguring his death and embalming. If you want to believe that these three gifts were actually given that is fine, but by not being tied to a literal interpretation you can go to a deeper level of meaning. As a final point, tradition has it that there were three magi simply because there were three gifts. This may not necessarily be the case. My wife, Lucy, is sometimes very generous and gives me three or four presents for Christmas. This doesn't mean that I have three or four wives! The converse is also true. Sometimes members of my family club together and buy me just one birthday present between them. The number of magi is not recorded in the bible. The number three arose largely because of the traditional carol, 'we three kings of Orient are'. I can almost hear you saying, Tom, that it doesn't matter how many there were.

Perhaps it doesn't. Maybe there weren't any! It certainly seems strange that three important people turned up apparently without any kind of retinue. I also wonder what happened to the three gifts. By introducing these men from the East, Matthew is saying that the gospel is not only for the Jews but also for non- Jews, the gentiles. At the end of his gospel he exhorts the disciples to go into all the world to preach and to baptise.

I hope you will enjoy Christmas even more after these explanations. It is a wonderful time to think about the significance of the birth of Jesus. Our calendar is dated from his birth; history changed because Jesus was born. Some say that Christmas is not the same when you are grown up and it is a festival just for children. Christmas is enjoyed in a different way when you are older. You appreciate even more the meaning of unconditional, sacrificial love and the hope that Jesus brings for a better world. If only people could learn to love as Jesus loved. The problem is that many people just turn up for the Christingle service and that is it for another year. To me, that is like turning up at an airport to go on holiday but staying in the departure lounge. How much fun would that be?! Christmas is but a departure point, and the real excitement lies in the journey and taking off from the celebration runway.

Blessings, Malcolm

p.s. If love is only for Christmas, what are we doing the rest of the year?

WHY DID JESUS DIE?

Dear Malcolm, Your last email has left me reeling. I assumed the Christmas stories were completely historical. I am still trying to get my head around some of the things you said. You have clearly based your thoughts on well-known biblical stories, so I must now reflect on your interpretations. It is just that I have taken so much for granted about Christmas without really giving it much thought. You have stimulated me to do a bit more reading around the subject but I think it is entirely possible to go to a deeper meaning even if you accept the stories as historically true. For example, I have heard many sermons about the meaning of the gifts the magi presented. These sermons have validity whether or not the event actually happened as recorded my Matthew. I guess my main criticism is that you are in danger of removing all the specialness of the birth of

Jesus and the fact that 'nothing is impossible for God' as Luke writes in chapter one.

Moving on from the birth of Jesus, I have three questions for you. I have been wondering why Jesus had to die. Sadly we all have to die but why was he crucified? Crucifixion is such a horrible, painful death. Was it really necessary? I know some people say he died for us and to forgive our sins, but I find it very difficult to believe the death of someone so long ago has anything to do with me. Certainly I believed it all when I was a student but, as I have said, doubts have now set in.

Hi Tom, many apologies for leaving you 'reeling', it was certainly not my intention. I was simply trying to encourage you to examine the biblical texts more closely. Such study brings its own rewards – a deeper understanding of Jesus. Of course, you are right, it is possible to go to a deeper meaning from whatever standpoint you study the text. My own feeling is, as I said, if the texts are taken at face value then they are in danger of being relegated to the level of fairy stories. Nothing could be further from the truth. I would certainly agree that the birth stories have a specialness and mystery all of their own. They are wonderful and have inspired people of all ages for hundreds of years.

Your text about nothing being impossible for God is interesting. Can God make a square into a circle? Well, some people do argue that God can work outside the natural laws of science and perform miracles. We will talk about miracles at a later stage but for the moment I want to affirm that miracles can happen if we allow the love of God to work in and through us. God only wants what is best for us and we can achieve far more than we think if we let the love of God into our lives.

Now let's look at your question. It is certainly historically true that Jesus was crucified but why did it happen? As you rightly say, some people say Jesus died so that all the wrong things we have done in our lives can be forgiven. This is mentioned in various places in the New Testament. The idea is that we have all done wrong things and in order to be forgiven by God, we have to offer a sacrifice. In the Old Testament, people used to offer up to God an unblemished lamb as a sacrifice to cancel out their sins. In the New Testament Jesus is regarded as the perfect, unblemished 'lamb', and therefore he is the person to be sacrificed to make up for our wrongdoings. The problem is that this has become the one interpretation of Jesus' death that people have fixated on, forgetting that there are other New Testament interpretations. Time doesn't allow me to go into all these but if you look on google you will see, for example, seven theories of the atonement summarised.

The idea of offering a body up for sacrifice is not something with which we are familiar. Yes, we know about people making sacrifices. You, for example, make sacrifices for your children. You go without things so they can benefit. People sometimes die saving somebody else. I saw a headline the other day 'father dies in rescuing his son from the sea', but that is quite different from saying 'father requires son to die in order to save others'. That would make God some kind of ogre who kills his own son; this is not the kind of God I believe in.

As you know, if I am not taking a Sunday service I usually attend my local Methodist church. I was in church a few weeks ago and the congregation were lustily singing a hymn. The first verse was very affirming and uplifting but then in the second verse I became confused. We all sang 'till on that cross as Jesus died, the wrath of God was satisfied'. I felt quite disturbed, so much so that I couldn't sing those words.

If God is so angry the only way to assuage his anger is to crucify his son then that is not the God I know or want to know. That kind of God comes from another century and a particular interpretation of the death of Jesus. Today, if a father nailed his son to a cross, for any reason whatsoever, he would be arrested and thrown into prison for murder and child abuse. For me, God is a God of love and I don't see this act as a loving thing to do. If we take it literally, there is the implication that God only forgives if there is an adequate sacrifice. This, however, places a limitation on God's power. I believe God loves us all without hesitation and that love is present long before the birth of Jesus – or his death.

For me God is pure love. The only biblical definition of God is 'God is love'. (1 John 4:8) Therefore it is theologically impossible for God to do anything other than love. In Jesus we see this love briefly lived out. Jesus is commissioned by God as an act of love to show us a way of life, not to engage in some kind of sacrificial transaction. God's love cannot be limited. We are actually forgiven though the grace of God, a complete free gift. Indeed, forgiveness is present long before the death of Jesus. For example, the psalmist writes 'if you, O Lord, kept a record of sins, O Lord, who could stand? But with you there is forgiveness.' (Psalm 130)

Jesus was killed because he came into conflict with the Jewish religious authorities. He was rumoured to be God's son and that was complete blasphemy to the religious leaders. He also forgave sins. An example would be in Matthew's gospel chapter 5 where Jesus says to a paralytic, 'take heart, son, your sins are forgiven'. It was thought that only God could forgive sins. Furthermore, the Jewish authorities placed great emphasis on obeying the law of the Old Testament, in particular, the Ten Commandments. Jesus, however, said the only important law was to love God and your neighbour as yourself. Nothing else mattered. No wonder the Jewish leaders found him difficult. He was challenging all they stood for and giving the Jewish people a taste of religious freedom instead of being constrained by ancient laws.

Jesus was also seen as a threat to the Roman leaders. We know that Palestine, the country where Jesus lived, was controlled by the Romans. The Roman Empire extended far and wide. Jesus preached about a kingdom he called the Kingdom of God. This was seen as a direct challenge to the Romans and their empire. Jesus was passionate about God, and what life would be like if

God were in charge of the world. No wonder he was killed.

The fact he died on a cross was very significant because a verse in the Old Testament states, 'anyone hung on a tree is under God's curse'. (Deut. 21:23) This was the way criminals were dealt with, totally vulnerable, in public view and cursed by God. It was a dreadful way to die, on a tree, or cross. As you say, Tom, it is a horrible painful way to die, in fact, human torture. If Jesus had died of some kind of contagious disease my guess is that his death would not have had the same impact or meaning. I also think that if he had just been seen as a prophet, or healer, or teacher he would not have been killed. How he would have died in that case, is anyone's guess.

Your third question is whether the death of Jesus was necessary. There is a very glib answer to this question. We all have to die, we are all terminal. Jesus is no exception. However, I don't think Jesus thought the purpose of his life was his death although this is open to question. After all, if he hadn't died there would have been no resurrection. As I have said, his death was the consequence of proclaiming a new kind of Kingdom. Jesus undoubtedly knew his life could have fatal consequences but this did not deter him. He persisted with what he believed in.

Tom, it seems to me we have entered some very deep water in this email. The important thing is that the sacrificial interpretation of the death of Jesus is only one interpretation. As I have said, there are others. It is very difficult to understand how the death of someone over 2000 years ago can have any relevance for my life, or your life, today. Suffice it to say, the impact of Jesus's death is still being felt to this day not only in my life, but all over the world. How many movements have begun with the death of their leader?

Blessings, Malcolm.

NEW LIFE?

Thanks Malcolm for your reply. I found it very helpful although not all Christians would agree with you. I was brought up to believe Jesus died for everybody's sins, and we often sang hymns to celebrate the fact. To realise there are different interpretations of the cross has come as something of a revelation, and a liberation. So thanks again. However, I'm not at all sure I agree with you when you say that God doesn't work outside of natural laws. Indeed, you contradict yourself. On the one hand you say God cannot be limited by requiring Jesus to be sacrificed before God can forgive. On the other hand you say God is limited because he can't make a circle square. I also think you have omitted a central meaning of the cross. The pain and suffering of Jesus's crucifixion can somehow help to reconcile me to God. For me it brings comfort that Jesus knew what it is like to be in intolerable pain. I don't feel so alone in my pain and suffering. Could this be another reason for Jesus's painful death? Anyway, that is not the main reason for writing again. At the heart of the Christian faith is the resurrection. It is a real stumbling block for me. Did Jesus really rise from the dead? I find this event very difficult to believe.

Hi Tom, many thanks for your thoughtful reply. You are absolutely right. I have contradicted myself on how God acts. I did say I don't know all the answers! For the moment let's leave it there. As I said, it brings into question the whole nature of miracles.

I heartily agree with your point about the crucifixion. How could I have overlooked it? Many times I have gazed at the cross and found there, paradoxically, peace. The mystery of the cross is that although a place of great suffering many have found it a place of healing. There is also great comfort in knowing that Jesus can somehow share in any suffering we may undergo.

Now let me try to answer your question about the resurrection. To be absolutely honest I find it difficult as well. Mind you, that doesn't mean it didn't happen. There are lots of things I don't understand. For example, computers have become an essential part of life but I haven't a clue how they work, and yet here I am writing this email to you on mine.

There are difficulties if we think Jesus rose bodily. In the New Testament gospels, sometimes he was recognised and sometimes not. Two disciples on the road to Emmaus did not recognise him (Luke 24:13ff) and on another occasion the disciples thought they were seeing a ghost; (Luke 24:37) Jesus seems to walk through closed doors and then, seemingly, disappear into thin air. "Although the doors were locked, Jesus came and stood among them." (John 20: 19 and 26) I wonder what clothes he would have been wearing.

My main problem with a bodily resurrection is what finally happened to Jesus' body? Yes, I know there is an ascension story when he disappeared into the clouds in full view of the disciples but what does this mean? Surely that is meant as a metaphor rather than fact. Did his body defy gravity and is now somewhere in outer space, beyond the Milky Way. Some people certainly believe in a bodily resurrection, but that seems to be more like resuscitation rather than resurrection.

What then is resurrection? Clearly, something dramatic happened. The disciples were very frightened after the crucifixion of Jesus. They thought that the Romans and the Jewish authorities would be searching for them, so they kept well hidden. Can you imagine how sad they must have felt? Their leader, the one they had followed for over two years had been brutally tortured and killed in front of everybody. They must have been in total despair; not only that, they had given up their livelihoods to follow him. What was to become of them?

There is no doubt in my mind that the disciples had a dramatic experience of Jesus. They were transformed and felt Jesus was alive in them. They realised they could carry on his teaching because Jesus was empowering them; they were now able to preach and teach and were no longer frightened. The change in them was amazing. Some were even prepared to be martyred; they refused to say 'Caesar is Lord', because for them Jesus was Lord. Some were executed or thrown to the lions. For the first followers of Jesus, he was a reality that nothing could destroy. The growth of the early church is testimony to this fact. The first Christians changed the society where they lived. They shared what they had amongst themselves, gave to the poor, and welcomed new comers. You can read in Acts how the early disciples 'turned the world upside down'. (Acts 17:6)

People today perform extraordinary acts of love and self-sacrifice because they believe wholeheartedly in Jesus. Even in this day and age, Christians in some parts of the world are being persecuted because they are Christians. Can you believe it? These acts of faith say more to me about the resurrection of Jesus than what actually took place on the first Easter.

The important point is how much of Jesus is alive in me? Some people concentrate on the cross of Jesus. This is a very potent symbol and a great consolation especially when we are going through a difficult and painful time. However, Jesus came so that we might enjoy life, life in all its abundance. Isn't that Good News?

As ever, yours, Malcolm.

p.s. When in doubt always choose the course of action that is life giving. Why choose something that is deadening?

ABUNDANT LIFE

Dear Malcolm, I'm so excited. We have just had a new addition to our family, a baby girl. She is wonderful and, of course, she looks just like her Mum! We are calling her Louise. I know this is unusual but my mother was called Louie and my mother in law was called Luise and so by the addition of one letter to the two names, we have Louise. That is my important bit of news but let me reply to your email.

I was confused with your line of thinking that Jesus's resurrection was a metaphor rather than a witness account of the disciples. I presume this is because you don't believe in miracles and God doesn't go against natural laws so bodily resurrection is unlikely or not possible? Isn't it just as big a leap to say that this means this is a metaphor than to believe that the son of God who came into the world, lived, changed lives, performed miracles, challenged cultural norms, died and rose again: He is not here, He has risen! (Luke 24:3-6) If that is the case, what do you think actually happened on Easter Sunday?

Also some Christians may think that you are taking some verses especially Luke 24 out of context to support your perspective that Jesus could not have risen bodily. For example, there may be many reasons why the disciples were 'kept from recognising him'. They thought they were seeing a ghost but a ghost doesn't have flesh and bones! Furthermore if Jesus's body was transformed he could certainly walk through closed doors. Not only that, I think the ascension then makes sense and, of course, our bodies will be transformed when we die as Paul says in 1Cor 15:50-53.

Of all your emails, I have found this the least easy to understand what you want to convey. What do you actually believe and what do you think happened to the body of Jesus?

Dear Tom, you have sent a very challenging reply. Many thanks. The resurrection of Jesus always raises lots of questions and far better brains than mine have wrestled with it. I don't think I likened it to a metaphor. If, as an act of faith, one takes your line that Jesus's body was miraculously transformed then, I have to agree, some of my difficulties disappear. However, my contention is that the biblical accounts are not historical accounts in the way that we record history. They are gospels and therefore written with the purpose of encouraging people to believe in Jesus as the Son of God. To which you will reply that, if the stories of Jesus are all made up then what is the point. Well, I don't like the idea of stories being made up either. Clearly there are historical events in the bible. Undoubtedly Jesus suffered and was crucified. I feel sure that he was also betrayed and denied. However, when we want to make a point we sometimes exaggerate and maybe get confused with details especially if we are remembering an event of years ago. The gospels are no different.

The earliest gospel, Mark, says nothing at all about the resurrection appearances. We simply read that the women who went to the tomb were afraid to say anything to anybody. The earliest and most reliable manuscripts of the gospel end there. In Matthew's gospel the women meet the risen Jesus who says 'tell my brothers to go to Galilee; there they will see me.' (Matt. 28:10) In Luke there is a more physical appearance firstly in the Upper Room in Jerusalem, and then on the road to Emmaus. The latest gospel, John, relates the story of your namesake Tom. This experience, as you know, is even more physical. Jesus says to Thomas, 'put your finger here, see my hands. Reach out your hand and put it into my side. Stop doubting and believe.' (John 20;27) There is also an extended account of the empty tomb and a conversation with Mary in the garden. It is as though there is a gradual change in the course of time from believing in something spiritual to something physical.

You clearly disagree with my comments about the road to Emmaus incident but it makes more sense to me to treat the story as a parable rather than a historical incident. Yes, it could have happened as written but I have difficulty in believing in a body comprised of flesh and bones which suddenly disappears like a magic illusion. I find it more helpful to realise that the spirit of Jesus becomes present when friends 'break bread' together, that is, share a meal. The incident is a powerful example of the importance of hospitality. As they shared a meal 'their eyes were opened.' They realised the spirit of Jesus was alive in them.

I have to be honest. I remain agnostic as to the precise details of the first Easter Sunday. I know, for some, the resurrection as a miracle can be a stumbling block. Is it important what happened to Jesus's body? For me, it is more beneficial to look at the effects of the first Easter. What is an indisputable fact is the first disciples were transformed from being a frightened group of individuals who had lost their charismatic leader into a dynamic, dedicated group bent on proclaiming a new way of life which could only be described as a risen life. This life entailed a self-sacrificial way of loving and was so radical a spark was ignited which subsequently spread throughout the world. This happened. It is beyond question.

What wonderful news. Many congratulations. No wonder you feel excited. I always get excited when I look at a new born baby. To see all the little toes and fingers perfectly formed is just wonderful. How we survive our journey into this world I will never fully understand, and when we emerge our lungs immediately start to function and we become independently functioning bodies. Amazing. The design of the human body is incredible, everything is so finely balanced. Our brains contain ten thousand million nerve cells with trillions and trillions of interconnections.

I know we have robots that can do all kinds of complex tasks, but the human brain takes some beating. I often wonder when I am out walking or jogging how quickly the brain reacts to an obstacle. Maybe it's a puddle I want to avoid, or a kerb I need to step over. As soon as I see the obstacle, my brain automatically computes the length of stride I need to take. All this is done without thinking. Take another example. Have you ever touched something very hot? Notice how you pull your hand away very, very quickly, even before your brain has told you the object is hot. Teaching robots to do these apparently simple tasks are proving extremely difficult. One job that we aren't very good at is opening doors. How many times have you tried to push a door open when the sign on the door quite clearly says 'pull'?!! Who knows why we do that?

Anyway, I seem to be rambling on because of the birth of your daughter. But it does give me the excuse of talking about life. You may not believe this but the word life is used many times in the New Testament. Let me give you a few examples from John's gospel.

I am the resurrection and the life.

I am the bread of life.

I have come that you might have life and have it in all its abundance.

I am the way, the truth and the life.

Of course, these quotes refer to Jesus and you could well argue that they have nothing to do with you. Your life, at the moment, consists of changing nappies and sleepless nights. My contention is that Jesus is concerned with all aspects of our lives. Christianity is a religion that is very much about how we live our daily lives although, of course, other religions offer a way of life as well. We need to maximize activities which stimulate a zest for living, maybe physical activities such as walking, gardening or involvement in sport. Maybe listening to music, sitting in the garden and observing the wonders of nature or looking up at the star filled sky and wondering or singing your favourite hymn in worship. Different things energise different people and you can only speak for yourself. How often do we find ourselves doing things that dull our enthusiasm for life? In fact, some of the things we engage in can be quite deadening. For example, sometimes I watch a television programme hoping it will improve. When I look back on the programme, if I'm being honest with myself, I have to admit it was quite a deadening experience. I had hoped it would improve but it didn't. Why didn't I switch it off? I guess it was sheer apathy or laziness. A useful exercise is to spend some time reflecting on what in our lives brings us enjoyment and what makes us downhearted.

A good way of doing this is at the end of a day before you go to sleep. Look back over the day and think about some of your experiences. What did you feel good about? Did you ever feel sad, helpless or angry? Try and discover what made you feel like that. For what experiences are you most grateful? For what experiences are you least grateful? When was today's high point? When was today's low point? Where was God's spirit present? Where was God absent? If you want to follow this idea up I recommend a book entitled 'Sleeping with Bread, holding what gives you life' by Dennis, Sheila and Matthew Linn. It is very readable and not very long.

Presumably you are very happy as an engineer but if ever you struggle over what direction you want to go in your life, try looking back over each day and get a sense of those experiences for which you can be really grateful. If you do this over a period of time, say a month, you will begin to get an idea of what you want to do with your life. Hopefully, you are already doing those things which bring you energy, satisfaction and life. This is what God wants us all to do, experience abundant life although in reality we know this is difficult for people living in countries where poverty, malnutrition and unrest are commonplace. I have no doubt that is what God wants but it does leave open the question of how one enjoys abundant life if you have been victimised, or abused or lost loved ones through war. I look back over my life and sometimes it has been extremely difficult to experience 'life in all its abundance'. On the other hand, many of the activities I have pursued have been rewarding, energising and life giving.

I must go now. I have a service to prepare for Sunday. I hope you are enjoying your baby daughter and not having too many sleepless nights. I wonder if she is going to be christened.

As ever, Malcolm

p.s. For what moment today am I most grateful?
For what moment today am I least grateful?

WHEN DISASTER STRIKES

Dear Malcolm, I can't go along with all you say. Why can't the resurrection be both a transformed physical bodily resurrection as well as a spiritual resurrection? Isn't that possible?

I also wonder what it is about Jesus that is so important. After all, there have been other charismatic leaders, Ghandi, Mandela and the Dalai Lama to name just three. Why not follow them? Furthermore, it's all very well talking about abundant life, but what about those people who through no fault of their own have been caught up in catastrophic events. I was watching The News the other day. There had been an earthquake in Italy, floods in Indonesia, and the war in Syria is just going on and on. Why do these catastrophes occur? What about insect pests and diseases that destroy our food crops? Why doesn't God do something about them? On a more personal level, one of my friends has just been diagnosed with cancer.

Dear Tom, as ever, many thanks for your challenging reply. I'm afraid we shall have to disagree with our views on the resurrection, but hopefully we can still be friends. As for other charismatic leaders, yes, I agree, there have been others, but I can only say that Jesus is the one for me. I find in him an inspiration that I have tried to emulate all my life. He shows us a radical way of life; one that is based on sacrifice and abundant love. Jesus actually lived the life he proclaims. There is no doubt in my mind that Jesus has a special connection with God that can only be described in terms of a father-son relationship.

The questions you are asking provide the stumbling block that many people find when questioning their faith. Life is just not fair. I sometimes play snakes and ladders with my grandchildren. One minute all is going well because they have ascended a few ladders and then, suddenly, at the throw of a dice, they find themselves hurtling down a snake. 'It's not fair grandad, I was winning but now I'm losing'. Shakespeare in Hamlet talks about the 'slings and arrows of outrageous fortune' and Jesus says God 'makes his sun shine on the evil and on the good, and sends rain on the righteous and on the unrighteous'. (Matt. 5:45)

I've just been watching the news and seen dramatic scenes of flooding in Indonesia you mentioned, and the earthquake in Italy. A few weeks ago there was the horrific fire in Grenfell tower in London, and before that a terrorist bomb in the Manchester arena. People were killed and badly injured because they were in the wrong place at the wrong time. Why doesn't God stop such awful things happening? Just think of those unlucky people in the Manchester arena who were in the bomb blast that went off after the concert. All they wanted to do was enjoy themselves and listen to their pop idol. You will know her name, but I hadn't heard of her. Or think about the terrorist incident on Westminster Bridge when a van ran into innocent people. A policeman was present who had his photograph taken with a tourist and an hour later he was dead. What heart ache for his family and loved ones.

A lot of bad events happen because of the evil intentions of humans or because of human stupidity. For example, some health problems arise because we don't exercise enough, consume unhealthy foods, drink too much alcohol, smoke tobacco, or take illegal substances. People have to take responsibility for their own actions. I can sense you saying, why doesn't God intervene so that death and self-destruction are prevented. Unfortunately, Godly intervention would result in a very unpredictable world.

Suppose you banged your head against the wall and it suddenly became soft so you didn't hurt yourself, or you accidentally put your hand in a flame but it didn't burn your skin. It would be a very strange and unpredictable world if this really happened. I realise that some philosophers and psychologists would disagree with me but I do believe that we all have a degree of freedom.

Yes, we have all been conditioned by our early upbringing but the bottom line is we can all make choices, God has given us freedom. The alternative is that we behave like pre-programmed machines or puppets on a string. I find that very hard to swallow. However, given that we all have some freedom then the consequence is we have to take responsibility for our actions. Of course, we can also suffer from the actions of others towards us. Trauma would be a good example.

I speak from personal experience. You may not know this, but quite recently my youngest son took his own life. I and the family were left in a state of total shock and desolation. The reality is that God did not step in and repair brain damage even though many prayers were offered. My son has to take responsibility for his own tragic action and we all have to live with the consequences. God does not wave a magic wand to take the pain away but he does promise he is with us in the midst of it. God knows what it is like to suffer – witness the crucifixion of Jesus – and therefore can empathise with us in our suffering and grief. I found it helpful, to know that someone understands. Jesus weeps with those who weep.

However, when you ask about earthquakes and tsunamis, so-called natural disasters, they need to be dealt with quite differently. Where do I start? I'm quite sure God does not want people to suffer or be in pain but there are some advantages of feeling pain. I was watching a television programme a few days ago, and a little girl who couldn't feel pain was interviewed. You might want to say 'lucky her'. The trouble is she kept damaging her body and she didn't know it.

For example, if she put her hand in boiling water she didn't feel any pain, so her hand came out with blisters on it. If she banged her head against the wall she didn't notice that she had a big bruise. She kept getting herself into all sorts of difficult situations and her parents had to keep an eye on her all the time. The point I am making is that pain has an important function. It tells us that something is wrong. It is a warning to stop what we are doing. If you go to the doctor the first question asked is, 'where is it hurting?' If you don't know, it is very difficult for the doctor to treat you.

I have still not really answered your question about natural disasters which cause so much pain and human misery. The world has been set in motion and it actually obeys basic scientific principles. You know that. The world is very predictable. You can buy tide timetables for years in advance. Evening follows day – every day! The sun doesn't suddenly decide not to shine, although we haven't seen much of it lately. We couldn't begin to send rockets into space if the planets didn't move with great predictability. The date of the next solar and lunar eclipses can be known many years in advance. Earthquakes happen because of the specific movement of tectonic plates. We are still striving to understand what creates tsunamis. As soon as we do, we will be able to predict them. Catastrophes are part and parcel of creation. God is not going to change what has been created any more than God is going to make a circle square. The world has been created with the freedom to evolve. In the past the UK was joined to France, the ice age sculpted valleys and lakes, our coastline is constantly changing.

It could also be argued that much suffering is caused by our own ignorance and, sometimes, folly. Pompeii was destroyed by volcanic eruption but the human suffering was exacerbated by the proximity of the city. Tsunamis cause suffering because too many people live on the coast and, furthermore, the tourist industry is based there. Historically big waves did little damage. Hurricanes destroy infrastructure because African houses are shacks, earthquakes destroy poorly constructed buildings due to cost cutting. Naples may be wiped out when Vesuvius blows again.

A final thought is that when people are caught up in a disaster the public generally respond with great compassion and send gifts of money, food, blankets and clothing. The young football players trapped in a cave in Thailand were rescued by a team of international divers. Doctors, nurses and others volunteer, for example, to go to areas of Africa infected with the ebola virus to help alleviate the suffering. Disasters can happen to anyone of us, therefore we respond generously.

You mentioned that your friend has been diagnosed with cancer. I was very sorry to hear that, and I hope you will be able to support him through a very stressful time. Thankfully, medical science has progressed so much, there are now many treatments for the cure of cancer. One day I think it will be eradicated. In the meantime we are left with the perennial question. Why is this life threatening disease so difficult to eradicate?

The story of cancer began about 800 million years ago when single celled organisms joined together and triggered the evolutionary path to become multicellular animals. Growth of plants and animals is the result of cell division. This is carefully controlled by genetic materials in the cell's computer, or nucleus. When a flesh wound is healing new cells are produced, but cell division for tissue repair ceases when healing is complete. If the cell's computer malfunctions, cells may continue to multiply out of control. This may result in the production of tumours, cancerous growths. Sir Paul Nurse, who was awarded the Nobel Prize for his research into this field, says that 'cancer is a disease of cell division'.

Cancerous cells reproduce themselves in an uncontrollable way and eventually may take over the whole organism. They forget what they were originally programmed for by their genetic material, their division is out of control. The biochemical and physiological pathways that create our body organs can also lead to the development of cancerous tumours when the cell's computer is no longer correctly programmed, and so they reproduce themselves. Malfunction is known to be caused by radiation, but when cancer affects children the cause is frequently unknown. I read somewhere that 'growth for sake of growth is the ideology of the cancer cell'. If God repeatedly intervened to dispose of the nasty bits, then the process of evolution could be called into question, and scientific enquiry, as we know it, would be almost impossible. I hope what I am saying about evolution is correct. You probably know far more about it than I do.

I've completely forgotten who said it but somebody once wrote that it is difficult to bear suffering when you have faith, but it is even more difficult when faith is absent. The strange thing is that in my ministry, I have noticed when people go through a difficult experience; they often feel nearer to God. Their spirituality is deepened. I know this is not always the case. Sometimes the suffering is so debilitating that people can lose their faith. This is often because of an angry reaction against God. People don't grow spiritually when everything is going well, they grow in faith when facing problems, working through them and finding God in the pain. I hope this helps, but it is not an easy question to deal with. Perhaps your next email will have some good news in it.

LOL Malcolm

p.s. Just remember that nothing lasts for ever. Whether a situation is good or bad, it will change sooner or later.

WHEN LIFE GETS DIFFICULT

Dear Malcolm, I was intrigued by your last email and decided to ask a friend who knows a bit about neuro science. He says that we don't always have the ability to choose. Apparently brain scans have shown that when we are under threat our thinking brain shuts down and a fight or flight mechanism takes over. This is an automatic response and essential for survival. My friend says we can learn to notice them and then choose a different response if necessary but many people have not learnt this freedom to choose, indeed, it may not be easily accessible. She gives the example of rape victims going into 'freeze', not because they have given consent to intercourse but because their bodies have shut down in order to increase their chances of survival.

My friend also says that although we all sometimes

behave from a pre-programmed place because our ingrained brain pathways have been laid down in childhood or in trauma the good news is that we have brain plasticity which allows for new pathways to be formed but these need to be learnt and practised.

For me, personally, I am left wondering where God is in evolution. Has God created the world and left it to evolve? Is God sovereign over all creation or not? Where does that leave you and me? Have we been created by chance? Is God involved at all in my existence?

Dear Tom, many thanks for your comments – or do I need to thank your friend?! I found his comments about our freedom to choose, very enlightening. I completely agree. God has given us degrees of freedom so that we do not behave like programmed computers or puppets on a string. As your friend says, ingrained brain pathways laid down in childhood can be challenged and the good news is we have brain plasticity which allows for new ideas to be tested, learnt, and practised.

As for your personal questions, there is no evidence God maintains overall sovereignty for evolutionary pathways. A loving god would surely correct gene mutations which result in cystic fibrosis and haemophilia, and prevent the development of bacterial resistance to antibiotics. Yet, less harmful evolutionary changes through natural selection exist all around us. Foxes and seagulls adjust their lifestyles to urban environments, and many plants have successfully invaded toxic mine spoil waste following metalliferous mining. The vast diversity of animals and plants surely confirms a freedom to evolve in the absence of a godly dictator, although this of itself does not imply that God is absent. All we can say is that God clearly loves diversity!

For me there is randomness in our personal creation. Think about all the thousands of sperm having the opportunity to fertilise one egg among many. In such a random way we were created but having been created we have the choice as to whether we want to involve God in our lives. Do we want to become the person that God wants us to be? Do we want God to be sovereign in our lives?

I want to add something to my last email. The important thing for me is how we react when life gets difficult. Do we blame it all on God? Throw a tantrum, have a good cry, become angry or maybe all of these. I have often found that prayer is a good antidote when life gets difficult. Not that prayer is simply to be used in a crisis, but maybe I can say more about that later.

My daughter has an interesting quotation on her lounge wall. 'Life isn't about waiting for the storm to pass. It's about learning to dance in the rain'. In other words, life is what we do when we are up against it, when the chips are down. As a family, when I was young we used to play whist. When my Mum picked up her cards you could always tell if she had been dealt a bad hand. She used to pull a face and groan. When she had a good hand, she never said a word. She kept very quiet.

In life, we have all been dealt, as it were, a hand of cards. We have to play to the best of our ability the cards we have been given. Sometimes, even when we think we have a bad set of cards, they can turn out to be a winning set, depending on how they are played. If we are playing with a partner their hand can be very helpful as well. Talking of cards, I saw a man on the television last night who had been born without any hands, but he was a magician! It had taken him a whole year to learn how to shuffle a pack of cards. Unbelievable. Most tasks are possible when you put your mind to them.

One of my favourite stories is in a book called 'Mastering Sadhana' by Carlos Valles. The book is about my favourite author Anthony de Mello.

A farmer had an old horse for tilling his fields. One day the horse escaped into the hills, and when the farmer's neighbours sympathised with the old man over his bad luck, the farmer replied, "Bad luck? Good luck? Who knows?" A week later the horse returned with a herd of wild horses from the hills, and this time the neighbours congratulated the farmer on his good luck. His reply was, "Good luck? Bad luck? Who knows?" Then, when the farmer's son was attempting to tame one of the wild horses, he fell off its back and broke his leg. Everyone thought this was very bad luck. Not the farmer, whose only reaction was, "Bad luck? Good luck? Who knows?" Some weeks later the army marched into the village and conscripted every able-bodied youth they found there. When they saw the farmer's son with his broken leg they let him off. Now was that good luck? Bad luck? Who knows?

The point of the story is that something which

appears to be bad on the outside may actually be good, and something that seems to be good may actually be bad. We need to find the good in the bad. This is not easy. One has only to think about rape and abuse, not to mention a terrorist atrocity. Christians believe that God doesn't want these terrible things to happen but strives to work with us to bring good out of the evil.

In this country we are very fortunate. Just think about the kind of 'hand' people have been dealt if they live in Syria, or places in Africa where there is no running water and barely enough food. The shelves in our supermarkets always seem to be full, even if there has been a poor harvest. We all have the chance of a good education and in the Western world most people live in comfort. How times have changed. My grandma left school when she was twelve and had to go to work in a cotton mill. If she wasn't there at 6 o'clock in the morning the gates were shut, she had no work and, therefore, no money. Furthermore, there was no National Health Service or sick pay, no central heating or indoor toilets. Life was very, very hard. As far as I know, though, she enjoyed life and experienced fulfilment in it. She was a devout Christian. An easy life and the acquisition of possessions are not always a source of happiness.

Of course, I don't want to underestimate how tough life can be for some people. They may be suffering psychologically, or physically, and just about hanging on. There have been times when I have been in survival mode and somehow just about coping. My spiritual advisor once gently chastised me by saying "thou shalt cope is not in the bible". In the bible is the belief that God's purposes are being worked out and nothing can separate us from that love. This is a statement of faith.

Lots of love. Malcolm

WHEN PRAYER GETS DRY

Dear Malcolm, I personally, find it very difficult to think of my life as random. If we have been created randomly, doesn't this take away all meaning to our lives? Why would we want to involve God at all if we have been created randomly?

By the way, many thanks for that De Mello story, it was very interesting. You also mentioned the importance of prayer. I have been thinking a lot about prayer lately, largely because, as I told you, my friend has cancer. Do you think God answers our prayers? What is the point of praying? If God knows everything then aren't we just telling God what God already knows? Do you pray? To be absolutely honest, my prayer life is almost non-existent. I have found the whole process to be dry and pointless.

Dear Tom, I think we will have to disagree on the question of randomness. It is clearly very important to you and all tied up with the sovereignty of God. For me, randomness does not take away our uniqueness. We are all special in the eyes of God and, as I said previously, it is our choice whether we let God into our lives and allow God to become sovereign. For this to happen, prayer becomes very important but that brings me to all your questions.

To be honest, I'm not sure where to start. Many books have been written trying to answer the questions you are asking. I'm afraid some prayers are like shopping lists or Christmas present lists. We tell God what we want and hope like Father Christmas, God will give us all we have asked for. Prayer doesn't function like that, God does not do tasks for us that we are perfectly able to do for ourselves. God did not help you to pass your exams all those years ago, you revised for weeks. Prayer helps to calm our anxiety and bring us to an inner peace. This helps us recall what we need to remember during an examination. I need to add the caveat that this depends on how we view God. If God induces fear and guilt in us then that is not going to be in the least bit calming.

There are stories of people being helped by the power of prayer. In some cases they have been cured of an illness. There are many other cases where, apparently, their prayers have not been answered. Sadly, people of all ages die from sickness, and those with spinal injuries remain paralysed. I have no idea how prayer works for some people but not for others. Many things happen even if I don't understand how. I will have more to say about praying for others in my next email.

You mentioned a sense of dryness in your prayer life. You are not alone, the thought that prayer is the last thing one wants to do is very common. I have often met people in my ministry who admit they never seem to find time to pray because there is always something more important to do. Prayer is not even on their daily agenda. It is not our wrongdoings that keep us distant from God, but our distorted images of God and also our hectic life styles; the desire to be doing something. I wonder why there is so much resistance to being in God's presence. Will God ask too much of me if I get too near? Will God still love me if he sees me as I really am? Perhaps, I had better play safe and keep my distance. In this way, we are tempted and the good becomes the enemy of the best.

Accepting God loves us is difficult to comprehend, yet it is the journey of acceptance we have to take. For some this is not easy especially if they have never experienced love in their own lives. We can only help them to access the God of Love by being loving towards them.

Prayer is not always accompanied by nice, glowing feelings. If they are present, all well and good, but more importantly prayer is about establishing a regular time when you can meet up with God. As with meeting a friend, these times can be very enjoyable and life giving, but at other times they are quite mundane. If you find that boredom has set in then a good plan is to change your routine. Indeed, try a different method of prayer or pray in a different place. Life would get very boring if we ate the same food every day. One method would be to read very slowly a biblical passage two or three times. You will alight on a particular word or phrase. Mull that over. What might God be saying to you in that word of phrase?

The other day I came across someone who said that praying was like sunbathing. All you have to do is turn up with your towel, deck chair and sun cream, and soak it up. The sun is there, albeit sometimes behind clouds, and there is nothing we can do to change it. In a similar way, the love of God is always there. All we have to do is turn up and make ourselves available.

If you find conversation difficult in prayer then just say 'thank you.' We can be thankful to have been born in this part of the world which is relatively untouched by water and food shortages or by civil war. Our weather is not usually extreme, nor do we live under a dictatorship. We are also blessed with freedom to live our lives more or less as we please without interference. You can stand up on Speaker's Corner in Hyde Park and express your own opinions on most subjects. One of my heroes, a Methodist Minister called Donald Soper, later Lord Soper, did precisely that every Sunday.

I want to say something about the Lord's Prayer because this has been the model for Christians since the time of Jesus and has been a symbol of unity for two thousand years. As I have said the world of the New Testament is quite different to ours, a world that

reinforces male authority and power and the Lord's
Prayer utilises both fatherhood and kingdom imagery.
In this way women can often feel marginalised, at the
base of a hierarchical pyramid. This divine being is also
'in heaven' and needs to be 'hallowed'. Some people
today find this concept of god as a supernatural heavenly
being who needs to be flattered very difficult, if not
impossible to believe. However, I have recently come
across a version which addresses God as Father-Mother,
Abba-Amma. I thought you might be interested.

Abba, amma: source from whom I came.
I reverence your name.
Your child indeed,
I pray you to meet my need
from your bountiful store:
neither less nor more.

I confess my need, the way I feed
my desires which then inflate my need.
blotting out care of the self and awareness of the other-
my sister, father, mother, brother.

Out of the largesse of your grace,
give us all a place
at your overflowing table.
Feed us, that we may become able
To quieten our own hungers,
Attend to others, both near ones and strangers.

May we so linger in love
at your banquet – no hurry to move-
until we are filled with your joy
Rising within and between us-pure, unalloyed.

This is more for private rather than public prayer but it is an example of transposing a well-known prayer into modern thought forms. It is in an article by Nicola Slee in The Journal of Theological Liberalism, volume 59, issue 3 if you want to follow this up.

You ask me Tom whether I pray. I like to begin each day with about half an hour of complete silence. Sometimes it's impossible because grandchildren might be staying and, as you know, not only do they get up very early, they can also be very noisy. I listen to the daily news while I'm having my breakfast and then I go into silence. No effort, no stress, no words, no music, just silence. For me, prayer is more like coming into God's presence, being very quiet, and, in a sense, allowing God to look at me and me to look at God. My spirit is trying to connect with the Great Spirit we call God. In a sense, prayer is an awareness of the love of God. Incidentally, this is not necessarily a holy kind of activity. We can often feel the love of God through music and art. I don't pretend this is easy because there are always distractions and, as I said, there is always the risk my mind will wander onto my daily routine. There seems so much to do and think about, even when you are retired.

That is my suggestion to you in all your busyness. Just find the time to listen.

As ever, Malcolm

p.s. More things are wrought by prayer than this world dreams of. (<u>Alfred Tennyson</u>)

PRAYERS FOR OTHERS

Dear Malcolm, it's all very well talking about listening in prayer but I don't find it at all easy. Anyway, aren't you being a little disingenuous? You have omitted to answer some important questions. Jesus said if we ask for anything in his name then our requests will be granted. (John 14:13) I mentioned that my friend has cancer. How do I pray for him? Does God answer our prayers? Anyway, what is the point of praying? If God knows everything what is the point of telling God what he already knows? Finally, although I agree with a lot of what you say, much of your thinking depends on how you envisage God.

Dear Tom, you have raised important questions. If we see God as a strict father figure who is ready to punish our every little misdemeanour then we are not going to spend much time with God, let alone ask God for anything. On the other hand, if we envisage God as a loving father who only wants what is best for us then all fear is banished and we will experience total acceptance in God's presence. 'Perfect love, casts out fear.'(1 John 4:18)

Certainly, for many people, listening is not easy. They have a strong Protestant work ethic. There is always something to do. Problems arise when our desire to do things keep us distant from God. Sometimes we use our busyness to drown out our difficult thoughts and painful feelings. For example, when I suffered the family tragedy I have previously mentioned, I found it very difficult to meditate on God without my thoughts wandering off to think about my son. On the other hand, as I have just mentioned, some people's image of God is not conducive to a healthy relationship.

Please note that some activities can help us get in touch with God. A walk in the country, or doing some gardening, or playing the piano can be very prayerful and energising activities. These are ways in which our minds are kept busy whilst our feelings can go to a different place and find God deep within us. I find that jogging is very helpful in this respect. I could say a lot more about being quiet but for the moment let me try to answer your other questions about prayer. My last email was really concentrating on contemplative prayer, but now you are asking what happens when we pray for other people.

An important point to bear in mind is not to make assumptions about the desires of other people. I heard a lady on the radio who has been blind from birth.

She becomes very upset when people of faith pray for her healing. Blindness is part of who she is. Or think about Jack who is a member of the church and is in hospital. He knows everyone is praying he recovers and can return home. This is not what Jack wants! He is ready to die and feels saddened everyone wants him to recover. There is always a danger in thinking we know what another person wishes. It is wise to ask if a person would like you to pray for them. When Jesus was confronted with a blind man asking for his help, Jesus asked 'what do you want me to do for you?' (Mark 10:51)

This problem is exacerbated if we believe God will select and answer our particular prayers. During the Second World War German and British Christians must have prayed for deliverance and peace. How can God respond to both sides of an argument? In the same way, we pray for a lovely sunny day in order to enjoy a family picnic without regard to the farmer who is desperately praying for rain. How can God answer both petitions?

Jesus asked us to pray 'in my name'. We are to ask only for those things which accord with God's love, but this assumes we know what this entails. Sadly, we frequently assume we know what God should do, and also that God has the power and will to act. We sometimes forget God has given us freedom and the responsibility to act for ourselves. Nowadays, most people have moved away from thinking God has a magic wand which can be waved at every whim that takes our fancy.

Does God answer our prayers? Think about your baby daughter Tom. As she grows up, are you going to give her everything she asks for? Of course not, precisely because you love her. You want to give her only items which you think are in her best interests. It is the same with God, only more so. I think it was C. S. Lewis who said every tombstone is a monument to unanswered prayer. We often don't receive a positive answer to our requests. This is not because we have not used the right words, given sufficient time to praying, or lack of faith, it is because God doesn't simply comply with our request.

This brings us to the implication of your email, how does God act? Does God intervene and bring about miracles? I went to school in Bolton and so I have always supported Bolton Wanderers football team. Last season they only just escaped relegation by winning their last game. The local newspaper reported it was a miracle. The word miracle can be used to describe many events. A religious miracle is one not explained by natural or scientific laws and, for a Christian it is usually attributed to God's intervention.

As I mentioned in my third email, God did not intervene to stop the Vietnam war, in spite of the numerous prayers that were offered. I joined the million people who marched against the invasion of Iraq. Tony Blair's government voted for military intervention; God did not intervene to stop a futile war. Yes, I know, 'futile' is a value judgement and you are free to disagree! Millions of prayers were offered to stop World War Two and the atrocities of the holocaust. Almighty God did not take any action, in fact, as I have said, the Germans thought God was on their side. On the belts of soldiers were the words, *Gott mit uns,* meaning 'God with us'.

The point could be debated but I think belief in an interventionist kind of God began to wane during the Great War. Good men endured the unspeakable horrors of the trenches. Thousands were slaughtered on a daily basis. God was implored to intervene but the terrible bloodshed continued, unabated. Apparently, God remained silent. If God is a God of love, why doesn't God do something about this tragedy?

Sadly, Tom, God is not going to intervene to remove your friend's cancer. I have no doubt, from a psychological point of view, knowing people are praying for both of you can bring a sense of well-being and calmness, but one prayer or a thousand will not stop cancerous cell division remaining out of control.

It is strange that our prayers of intercession seem to be mostly about people who have some physical condition. This is understandable but it tends to underplay the importance of our spiritual life. What could be more important than praying for people who see life as utterly meaningless, who live with a resentment or anger that is poisoning their life, who find it impossible to forgive someone, or who have become enslaved to a particular addiction. Surely these people are in great need of our prayers.

Ever since the compilation of the Church of England prayer book in 1662, the monarch has been prayed for.

Prayers are regularly offered for Queen Elizabeth that god will 'endue her plenteously with heavenly gifts; grant her in health and wealth long to live'. The Queen has certainly been blessed with a long life, but this was not the case with her father, George VI, or many monarchs before her.

Yet many people will testify to the power of prayer, it has worked for them. They or someone they know have been healed and doctors have no explanation. Christians interpret a spontaneous remission as a miracle from god, a rare event still used to determine sainthood in the Roman Catholic Church. My guess is that in the course of time, as medical science advances, explanations will be found and God will not be required. This has happened over the years, medical science has made tremendous strides into curing many physical illnesses. We no longer try to heal an eye malfunction with spittle as Jesus did, or with prayer, we go to an optician or ophthalmic surgeon. Epilepsy is no longer seen as the work of the devil but as a condition controlled by medication. We live in a completely different world to that of the New Testament. The result is God has been pushed more and more to the periphery of secular life styles. This is an injustice, for me, God is central to life, not on the edge. In fairness, I have to say that some scientists do not see God on the edge but absolutely in the centre. The more science reveals, the more they see of God.

A miraculous healing may be short lived, followed by patient deterioration. It then has to be accepted the claimed medical miracle was just a temporary remission from sickness.

Nevertheless, the bible and centuries of Christian experience testify to the fact that when God is brought into a situation through prayer, the effects can be very positive. Never mind that we don't exactly know how prayers work or what impact they have, the fact is we care about people, passionately, and we cannot help but express our love and concern for them before God. We instinctively commend people to God's care. Exactly the same happens when we see pictures of starving children, our heart goes out to them.

In this way, intercessory prayer involves identifying ourselves with the compassion of God; sharing with God our love and concern for others. Praying for relations, friends and neighbours is a way of loving them. Saying we will pray for someone is a serious commitment to loving a person enough to uphold them before God. Someone has said that praying for other people is like bringing them into a room in which God is already present. In other words, we are bringing them into the orbit of God's love and care. If praying somehow releases a feeling of God's loving presence in our lives, then why would we ever want to stop? It seems to be a natural human response to pray for someone. This is part of our love and concern for them, to ignore would seem to be quite mean and callous.

Hopefully, there is also a desire to respond, not just in words and platitudes but in actions, helping as far as we can to translate our prayers into deeds. If someone is ill, we could phone them, send a card or even pay them a visit to cheer them up. If we are praying for someone the process involves us and God. Prayer is not about us telling God what to do but finding the space so we are available to God who can then tell us what to do. In the last analysis, intercessions are about listening. In a seminal book on prayer called 'The Use of Praying', Neville Ward wrote, 'the Christian idea of intercession is that it is not a means we employ to persuade God to act in a situation he has presumably over looked or into which he needs to be summoned, but a means God employs to summon *our* help through our membership in the Body of Christ.'

As ever, lots of love, Malcolm

p.s. God is not going to do something for us that we are perfectly capable of doing ourselves.

Just Listen

Hi Malcolm, I'm not entirely convinced by what you say. I am still of the opinion that God does answer prayers although maybe not in the way we expect. Anyway, who are you to say whether God intervenes or not? Isn't that up to God? Furthermore, God asks us to be persistent in prayer. (Luke 11;5-10) In the asking and the persistence, don't we get to know God better?

Neither am I convinced about this listening you talk about. When I listen all I can hear is the television, a dog barking, cars passing outside and other noises. I am distracted with a torrent of thoughts going on inside my head; all the tasks I have to do, and all the tasks I regret doing. How do you listen with everything going on around you and inside your head?

Dear Tom, as ever, many thanks for your reply and your questions. You have very gently put me in my place. I am not trying to be God and I certainly don't know all the answers. To be absolutely honest I find all questions about whether God intervenes or not, very elusive to answer. If someone feels their prayer has been answered, then nothing more need be said. They are fully convinced God is in charge and has the power to change things. This is a matter of faith.

Whether God answers prayer or not I find very difficult to answer. There is certainly evidence to the contrary as I pointed out in reference to wars. You mentioned persistence in prayer and, yes, this helps us to know God better but there comes a time when enough is enough. Think about your daughter continually asking for the same thing and you know it is not good for her. The only answer you can give is a very definite 'No' although it doesn't stop her asking!

Let me deal with your other questions about listening. Nobody said praying and listening was easy!! Everybody finds it difficult. Think about all those examinations you took at school, and at university. You practised by revising past papers, and found your knowledge of engineering had greatly improved. It's the same with prayer, if you want to get better, you practise. As the well-known saying goes, practise makes perfect. Being quiet and listening helps you to connect with God in your heart, when your spirit meets God's spirit.

Incidentally, I read in the newspaper, some junior schools are encouraging their classes to have about five minutes silence every day. Apparently, all the children enjoy this and teachers report their class work is much improved.

There are some practical ideas you can try to make your quiet time a bit easier. For example, to help with your concentration, you could focus on a vase of flowers, a picture, or a cross, anything that helps to gain your attention for a few minutes. My favourite focus is a lighted candle. Doing this helps you to shut out all those distractions you wrote about. If there are noises you can't eliminate try not to fight against them. Another idea is to close your eyes and concentrate on your breathing. Don't change your breathing. Just notice yourself breathing in and out. Whenever you are distracted, just come back and focus on your breathing.

If neither of those ideas work for you, then, a third idea would be to keep repeating a word or phrase. Some people call this a mantra. I often use the words 'Kyrie Eleison', Lord have mercy. The phrase works for me, but the mantra doesn't have to be religious. What works for you is the important point.

The objective is to assist you to link with the God who is inside us. If you want to get to know somebody you spend time with them. That is what you do with your friends. It is the same with God. In fact, some people say that prayer is spending time with God, nothing more or nothing less. People worry about whether they are saying the right words in their prayers. As though God minds! Words have to be used sometimes, but this is a different kind of praying. No striving or worrying you are saying the right thing, just trusting we are accepted as we are. Why not give it a try. I recommend it. There are all sorts of online sites now, that can be used as a basis for daily meditation.

The Methodist Church has a whole collection of resources available; http://www.methodist.org.uk/prayer-and-worship/ Jesuits have a Pray as You Go app. http://www.pray-as-you-go.org/ You can also join a community praying online such as the Northumbria Community. (http://www.northumbriacommunity.org/offices/how-to –use-the-daily-office) There's really no end of resources on the internet. My preferred resource at the moment comes from the Centre for Action and Contemplation, http://www.cac.org/

The bible has plenty of references to silence. Here are just a few.

'Be still and know that I am God'. Psalm 46

'He leads me beside still waters, he restores my soul'. Psalm 23

'For God alone my soul waits in silence,

from him comes my salvation'. Psalm 62:1

As you know Elijah didn't find God in all the noise and turmoil of an earthquake, wind or fire but in the 'still small voice'. 1Kings19

Mother Theresa once said:-

'Let us adore Jesus in our hearts,

Who spent thirty years out of thirty-three in silence;

Who began his public life by spending forty days in silence;

Who often retired alone to spend the night in silence'.

Of course, long before Christianity, Buddhists have

practised the art of meditation. Nowadays meditation is also practised by many who would not subscribe to any particular faith. This kind of meditation is known as mindfulness, the psychological process of bringing one's attention to experiences occurring in the present moment. I recommend a book called 'The Miracle of Mindfulness' by a Buddhist monk called ThichNhat Hanh.

I hope, Tom, I've said enough to convince you of the importance of keeping quiet before God. I once went on a thirty day silent retreat but that is another story. Suffice it to say that it changed my life.

Blessings Malcolm

p.s. All the troubles of life come upon us because we refuse to sit quietly for a while each day in our rooms. Blasé Pascal.

RETREATING

Dear Malcolm. You have triggered my interest in your time spent on retreat. What is a retreat? It implies you are under attack and need to get out of the firing line as quickly as possible.

Dear Tom, I agree, it does sound like that, but in my case it's not because I have been at war with an enemy. For me, the escape was from the stress of everyday life. Sometimes the best plan of action for an army is to retreat so they can re-form and prepare for the next battle.

Over twenty years ago, my church offered me the wonderful gift of a sabbatical which meant no work for three months. Wonderful. But what could I do? I didn't want to stay in bed all day, watch constant television, do some gardening, read books or have an extended holiday in some far off sunny place. Some of my friends said they had been on a retreat and had found it very beneficial. I decided to investigate this for myself.

I found myself knocking on the door of Ladywell retreat centre in Godalming, Surrey. I had booked myself in for a thirty day silent retreat without having any idea what it entailed. I was allowed an hour's conversation each day with a Sister who was there to help and encourage me through the silence. I was not allowed any books, music, conversation, telephone calls, radio or television. Just silence. On the very first day I wondered how on earth I had got myself into this situation. Why was I there? I had a very strong, deep feeling that God wanted me to be there.

On the first day I went for a long walk. In the distance I could see a farm house which looked very interesting. I had nothing else to do so I decided to go and check it out. This meant walking around a lake, through some woods and over a field. Eventually I found myself standing outside the farm house. It looked quite interesting, in reasonable condition and well made. I stood and stared for a little while before realising the house was completely empty. Then the penny dropped. I suddenly realised why I was on retreat. I was completely empty. For approximately twenty years I had been very busy in ministry, running here there and everywhere. I was burnt out, and I was unaware there was nothing left inside. Only by getting away from the busyness of everyday life did I find the time and space to reflect on my life and the direction it was taking. The retreat provided me with space to reflect on my life and time to be with God. I can honestly say the retreat saved my spiritual bacon.

Retreats don't necessarily have to be silent but mine certainly was. I spent an hour each day in conversation with a Sister who lovingly supervised and directed my progress. Although I was unaware at the time, I was actually following the Spiritual Exercises of Ignatius Loyola. Let me tell you a little bit about this interesting person, Ignatius.

He was born in 1591 in the Spanish town of Loyola and was christened Inigo, although he later became known as Ignatius. As a soldier he was seriously injured and during convalescence he began to read the only books that were available. These were not romantic novels, but stories about the life of Christ and many saints. Convalescence was a major turning point in his life. Instead of dreaming about becoming a great warrior and winning the hand of some fair lady, he began to dream about following Christ. These dreams gave him a feeling of contentment whilst earlier dreams of deeds of chivalry left him sad and discontented. He concluded the dreams of Christ were inspired by God. Ignatius described his experiences in terms of good and bad spirits, it was this discernment that led to his conversion. Jesus Christ was now much more important than the Spanish king he had been serving.

After periods of time spent in isolation and a monastery his prayers became closely linked to gospel stories. He imagined he could be present at biblical events such as the last supper in order to observe and even talk to those present. Sometimes he experienced feelings of joy, on other occasions times of doubt. These experiences became known as the Ignatian Exercises. Ignatius shared these exercises with his friends who later became known as the Society of Jesus, or Jesuits.

This group of people in the first instance were nearly all laymen at the time of taking the Exercises. In other words, they were not designed for those who had taken to the Priesthood or were members of Religious Orders or for especially holy people. They were written for people who simply wanted to deepen their relationship with God and know, serve and love God better. I found the process extremely hard. On the first day of my retreat I found it very difficult to concentrate solely on spiritual events, my mind easily wandered. I thought there was no way I could last out for thirty days. The Sister guiding me advised to take each day at a time.

This is very good advice, especially if you find yourself going through a difficult period and you wonder if it is ever going to end. People very often feel like this, for example, when they have been bereaved, or divorced, or made redundant. How am I ever going to get through the next few days, let alone weeks? A very good idea is not to think too far ahead, but simply take things one day at a time. A very significant verse in the bible is 'do not worry about tomorrow, for tomorrow will bring worries of its own. Today's trouble is enough for today.' (Matt. 6:34) The preceding verses are also very helpful.

Using the spiritual exercises recommended by

Ignatius, or, for many people a period of silent prayer, offers a way to deepen your awareness of God, develop your spiritual discernment and move to a place of greater spiritual freedom. I learned, above all else, that God is in the present moment. We spend a lot of time planning for the future or remembering the past, and as a result we actually exclude God. The only moment in which God is available is the present moment. I learnt to appreciate the presence of God simply by 'being' rather than 'doing'. Silent prayer, apparently doing nothing, enables us to get in tune with our senses and feelings and it is here that our personal God is found, not so much in our cerebral processes.

I should mention my retreat consisted of five separate hours of prayer each day. For each session the Sister provided a biblical text for meditation. The retreat consisted of four distinct phases, meditating on sin, my own and the sins of the church, the life of Jesus, the events of Holy Week and finally, the Resurrection. When the Sister felt I was ready she moved me on to the next stage. There was a rest day in between each phase when the number of prayer sessions was reduced to three. From a practical point of view all my meals were provided, and one of the sisters was kind enough to do my laundry.

Although I retreated, and in a sense escaped from my daily life, when I returned home I was much more energised and able to fulfil afresh my responsibilities as a Methodist minister. My faith had been strengthened. If you are interested, I wrote a book about my retreat experiences entitled 'Journeying with God' and, obviously, it goes into much greater detail.

Of course not all retreats last thirty days. They are exceptional and, in any case, people don't usually have that amount of time, or money. An alternative is to work through these Spiritual Exercises in your everyday life without going to a retreat house. You would still need a companion to act as a guide. However, it can be very beneficial to go on a weekend retreat or, if possible, a longer one. As somebody once said, a retreat allows your spirit to catch up with your body. There are a variety of options in various retreat houses all around the country and there is a national organisation called the Retreat Association that can offer advice and suggest a possible guide. Perhaps you could take the plunge, Tom, and sign up for one. I can't promise you won't regret it but on many occasions I have seen people turn up for a retreat tired, anxious, stressed, if not completely burnt out, yet at the close of the retreat they have returned home refreshed in mind and spirit. Maybe God has been found in the silence.

As ever, Malcolm

p.s. Everyone needs enough silence and solitude in their lives to enable that deep inner voice of their own true self to be heard. (Thomas Merton).

WHY GO TO CHURCH?

Hi Malcolm, I was fascinated by your experience of retreat. I would like to know more about it; maybe I'll buy your book. Unfortunately, most people haven't the time or the money to go on retreat. They have to make do with their local church services. I know you go to church most Sundays. Why do you bother? Surely there are more exciting things to do. The last time I went to church the service was boring and the sermon irrelevant. The preacher's sermon had little or no relevance to my daily life.

Hi Tom, I agree, the church can actually turn many people away from the Christian faith. Church services are frequently unattractive, particularly to young people and I do sometimes wonder why I bother to attend. Some churches now include modern music with guitars and drums, but I'm not surprised attendance is poor, except possibly at Christmas. Interestingly, even if people don't attend a church they often want their children to go to a church school.

In order to make church services more relevant there is now a movement called Fresh Expressions of church. This seeks to establish new church formats, in order to engage with the majority of people who rarely attend places of worship. These patterns usually emerge when a small group of Christians decide to try to share their faith in a way that is meaningful for other people. One popular Fresh Expression is Messy Church, this is a form of church for children and adults that involves creativity, celebration and food. It is primarily for people who don't already belong to another form of church and meets at a time that suits people who don't already belong to church. Typically there is a welcome, a long creative time to explore a biblical theme through a messy creative activity, a short celebration time involving story, prayer, song and games and a sit-down meal together at tables. All elements include people of all ages, adults and children.

Churches are also experimenting with seating arrangements, church pews are no longer obligatory, services being conducted in comfortable chairs around tables; a relaxed Café Church ambience. New technology is often used in services so that not only is modern music available but also videos and visual images can be easily accessed. Power point presentations are becoming more frequent.

All these developments are, for the most part, good, but for me what is central to the message of Christianity is a community of people who are trying to be followers of Jesus. This is not an exclusive group. On the contrary, all are included. As you know, St. Paul called this the body of Christ. The first thing that Jesus did was to gather a community of twelve disciples around him. They were all men because the culture at that time was patriarchal and women were regarded as second class citizens although there is no evidence to suggest Jesus was against having female disciples. Indeed, the bible tells us that women were part of his community, helping to support Jesus in all he did. You can read about this in Luke's gospel, chapter eight.

Psychologists tell us that human beings are social animals; we are born to live and die within a community. The most supportive community is usually the family. Social isolation can destroy the human spirit, it has been used as a form of torture, although it is surprising that many people love their own space and choose to live alone. It is sad that many elderly people live very lonely lives, and are especially vulnerable to anxiety, cold weather, and a lack of conversation during the winter months. Loneliness is often a root cause of mental illness. Research shows that people who attend church usually live healthier and longer lives.

We now live in a world that has online communities, Facebook, Instagram and probably others that I haven't even heard of. I find it very difficult when I'm talking to someone if they are distracted by their phone which seems to be glued to their hands. Apparently, sending a text to someone or reading a text message is far more important than actually talking to someone face to face. There is a danger of people living in a virtual community.

At its best, the church is a place where all are accepted and loved and where people can feel supported. The church, after all, is people. The church is not a building but a community of caring people, an influence for good . They often organise playgroups, clubs for senior citizens, and social activities for young people. More recent projects include the setting up of food banks. These are run by volunteers and food is offered to the neediest in the community.

In my church I am on a rota to help out with a luncheon club. I spend the morning peeling potatoes and carrots, then serve lunch to elderly people from the local community. Many individual Christians are involved in charitable organisations and volunteer work in the community. Interestingly, Pope Francis has installed three showers and a barbers in the Vatican for homeless people, plus a free medical centre. Clearly, the church can be a force for good and many communities would be impoverished without them. Even today, some people still marry in a church, often have their children christened and want their funeral service there as well.

LOL Malcolm

p.s. If a live coal is plucked from a roaring fire, it very quickly loses its glow.

WHAT IS THE GOOD NEWS?

Dear Malcolm, Thanks for your thoughts about attending church. I take your point about many of them being deeply involved in the community, but I do wish their services could be more relevant to the world I live in. The hymns of Wesley do not resonate with me either. They were written in a different age and utilise completely different images and ways of thinking about the world. I remember singing heartily about the first born seraph. What does this mean, and what is its relevance to me? It certainly doesn't sound like good news. When I hear good news I become excited and want to tell everyone I meet, but I don't want to tell anyone about church.

Dear Tom, I am in agreement with you Tom. Church services may be irrelevant, divorced from the world I inhabit. Incidentally, if you want to know about the first born seraph I suggest you google it. I won't bore you with the details. Good news means different things to different people. For some it is very good news when they realise they are going to have a baby, as it was for you and your wife. For others, who have decided not to have a family, it is not good news if they become pregnant. For some it is good news if one particular party wins the general election, for the opposition it is definitely not good news. Some things, though, we can agree on. There are many events we know provide a feeling of joy. It is always good news when your children pass their examinations. You appreciated your graduation ceremony. Most people are thrilled when they win the national lottery, but that is something I have never taken part in so I wouldn't really know.

The question you are really asking is what is the Good News that Christianity speaks of? For some it means freedom, especially if they have been trapped in some kind of addiction, alcohol, gambling, or shopping. Their freedom is controlled by their addiction. Following the life of Jesus can release people from the addiction and give them back their freedom. 'You will know the truth and the truth will make you free.' (John 8:32) There is a Wesleyan hymn with these words, 'My chains fell off, my heart was free, I rose, went forth and followed thee'. Incidentally, it is the same hymn which mentions the first born seraph. For some, Good News means liberation from all that prevents us from enjoying life although, paradoxically, even if someone is suffering they may still enjoy life.

Some people can feel a sense of alienation; they just feel totally out of sorts with themselves, other people and the world about them. If they find the Christian faith it is like coming home to the place where they belong. In this sense, Good News means reconciliation; a sense of belonging and being loved. There's a sense of being loved in the biblical parable of the prodigal son. In the parable the son finds himself a long way from home physically and metaphorically. He decides to go home where he belongs, and his father welcomes him with open arms. When we feel cut off, or alienated, it is worth remembering that God is always waiting for us to return.

For many people Good News can be a glass of water or a piece of bread. The Good News is about loving our neighbour, helping them whenever we can, putting other people before ourselves and not being selfish, actually being bearers of Good News.

Sometimes people can feel really lost. They have no aim in life and become like a boat at sea that has lost its rudder; it moves wherever the waves take it. The Good News for drifters is that you discover what life can be like if you drop an anchor into the teachings of Jesus and no longer drift aimlessly through life, but have an aim and a sense of purpose. This sense of aimlessness is not to be confused with being laid back and simply taking what life throws at you.

For other people the Good News is about finding

wholeness and a sense of peace. This is a bit difficult, I know, but it doesn't necessarily mean being cured. It does mean finding wholeness. During my life I have met some lovely 'whole' people and yet they were confined to a wheel chair. For such people the Good News means finding in Jesus a sense of peace, wholeness and well-being although, I guess we all moan from time to time. I know I do! We are not angels or robots but we are all human.

For me, the Good News is very much about forgiveness for past wrong doings, acceptance of me with all my shortcomings and therefore a freedom to enjoy life with all its wonderful opportunities. So you see, Tom the answer to your question isn't as easy as you thought. The important thing is that you discover what the Good News might mean for you.

LOL Malcolm

p.s. God loves you because of who God is, not because of anything you did or didn't do. (Regina Brett)

THREE INTO ONE

Dear Malcolm, many thanks for your reply. Clearly the good news is different for different people but I need a little more explanation please. You refer to the fourth gospel and the truth that makes us free. What is this truth and how does Jesus release people from their addiction? Furthermore, I wonder what is the good news for people who are suffering?

Believe it or not I went to church last week. It was an effort I must confess, especially with our little baby. Apparently it was Trinity Sunday and we sang a hymn I couldn't get my head round. This was the final verse.

> Praise and honour to the Father,
> praise and honour to the Son,
> praise and honour to the Spirit,
> ever Three, and ever One,
> consubstantial, co-eternal,
> while unending ages run.

That is theological jargon, not to mention the mathematical riddle! How can a Father, Son, and Spirit exist as one entity? It feels a bit like two plus two equals five in George Orwell's nineteen eighty four where people have to believe all kinds of dogma if they want to belong to The Party.

Dear Tom, as ever many thanks for your reply. You have left me with some searching questions! 'What is truth?' is the very same question Pilate asked of Jesus prior to his crucifixion. He didn't realise the truth was standing before him. For me, as I try, with very faltering steps, to follow the example of Jesus I have glimpses into God and, therefore I believe, the truth about life. If I try to keep focused on the life of Jesus, I am freed from all that holds me back. I am reminded of the text in the book of Hebrews, ' let us also lay aside every weight and the sin that clings so closely, and let us run with perseverance the race that is before us.' (Hebs. 12: verse1)

I have written in a previous book 'Running the Race', how Paul likens the Christian life to running a race. Athletes need to train with great determination and perseverance if they are going to be successful. They have to forgo many activities which other people normally undertake. For example, they devote their lives to a strict training discipline and they are very careful about what they eat. Their focus automatically means they have to let go of everything that holds them back.

This kind of life is not easy, nor is the Christian

life. I often fail, and we all benefit from the help of others. For example, those suffering from alcohol addiction can attend A.A. meetings and follow their 12 step programme; a process which has many religious overtones. We all have habits that hold us back from following Jesus but for the Christian, the aim is clear. The more firmly we keep our eyes on Jesus the more likely it is that we shall be released from all that holds us back.

Your other question about suffering and good news is not easy to answer either. I can only repeat what I have said previously about meditating on the cross; a potent symbol of horrific suffering. This can somehow bring a sense of peace and calm. I cannot explain this rationally. I only know it works for me. This is love personified.

I hope this helps but let me now try to answer your questions about the Trinity. I agree, how people are expected to understand the hymn you mentioned baffles me, especially if they haven't been brought up to attend a weekly church service. It really does sound like dogma. Trinity Sunday is the day when we remember a doctrine, not an event such as Easter. I wonder if I can explain this mathematical riddle we call the Trinity which implies God is one and yet three.

As a scientist you know water exists as ice, water and steam, yet the three formats have the same chemical composition. I can be defined as a son, husband, and father, yet I am still just me. These examples are useful up to a point but as I previously explained we can only talk about God by analogy or metaphor but these fall short. The question remains, how precisely is Jesus related to God? Does Jesus relate to God in the same way that I relate to my father? Are God and Jesus composed of the same or a similar chemical substance?

The Greek word for 'same substance' is *homoiousia,* but the word for 'similar substance' is *homoousia.* There was a great argument during the 4th century about these two words. After much debating the early theologians concluded the first Greek word was the most appropriate, and concluded Jesus the son and God the father were one in being or of single essence. This implied Jesus was of the same substance as God the father. Incidentally, this is what the word consubstantial means, and it is one of the cornerstones of theology in the Nicene Creed. Today we could justifiably discuss precisely what is meant by substance. The controversy in 325 A.D. occurred because of only one Greek letter, an iota! These problems of vocabulary were clearly important to early theologians. This is where the idiom 'different by one iota' comes from. There is more historical intrigue; early Christians also fell out over the interpretation of a single word, as well as a single letter, their Filioque argument!

The filioque debate was, and still is, a controversy in the church in relation to the Holy Spirit. It is centred on the question from where the Holy Spirit emanated; the father, or the father and the son. The word *filioque* means "and son" in Latin, these two words were added to the Nicene Creed, indicating that the Holy Spirit proceeded from the father "and son." There was so much contention over this issue that it eventually led to the split between the Roman Catholic and Eastern Orthodox churches in A. D. 1054. The two churches are still not in agreement over the significance of this single word. The Eastern wing of the Church believed and still believes that the father alone had given rise to the Holy Spirit, and the idea that both father and son had done so, is regarded as heretical.

Clearly where the Spirit originates from is not an easy concept. Both churches use biblical texts to support their claim but I think it is futile for most people to discuss this. I find such arguments quite sterile. It may be heretical of me to say so but I believe truth is not locked for ever in the statements of the Nicene Creed. Why should we think the early church fathers and theologians hold a monopoly of truth and morality in the modern world? Doesn't God continue to be revealed and therefore doesn't truth continue to be discovered and interpreted in different ways in accordance with recent revelations? The Christian church has become blinkered and constrained by its adherence to ancient dogmas and creeds. It is now time to accept their presence may be partly responsible for the decline in church attendance in this country. Wouldn't it be good if we could reframe the creeds so they made sense to modern ears?

Although the bible doesn't specifically mention the Trinity as such there are clear indications God was thought of as the Creator, that Jesus lived, and the early

Christians, and Christians today, can feel empowered by the Holy Spirit. For the first disciples this experience of the Holy Spirit was felt at the resurrection of Jesus. In the fourth gospel when Jesus suddenly appeared to his disciples, are the words, "he breathed on them, and said to them, 'receive the Holy Spirit'". There is a strong implication that the resurrection experience and the reception of the Holy Spirit are one and the same event. Luke separates these events so the reception of the Holy Spirit is delayed for fifty days after Easter Day until the day of Pentecost.

The account of John makes more sense to me. There is God who is, as I have previously said, a mystery to be investigated, the person of Jesus, and the Holy Spirit which is the spirit of Jesus that lives on after his death. The theory is that these three aspects of God are co-eternal, in other words, they exist together for ever. Quite honestly I no longer lose any sleep trying to work out what this actually means. There are more important issues to deal with, for example, how do I love my neighbour as myself, can I forgive others, how can I actually be a disciple of Jesus in this day and age?

Many books have been written on the subject but the best I have seen is called 'The Divine Dance' by Richard Rohr. I'm going to finish with rather a long quote of his.

"The energy in the universe is not in the planets, or in the protons or neutrons, but in *the relationship between them.* Not in the particles but in the space between them. Not in the cells of organisms but in the way the cells feed and give feedback to each other. Not in any precise definition of the three persons of the Trinity as much as in the *relationship between the three!* This is where the power for infinite renewal is at work:

The loving relationship between them.

The infinite love between them.

The dance itself."

I hope this explanation hasn't totally confused you. Some people relate to God as father/mother, others relate to Jesus, whilst the remainder prefer to relate to the Holy Spirit, all three are expressions of God. Another way of thinking about this is God as love maker, God as pain bearer and God as life giver. You take your pick but the important thing is they are all of God.

Yours, as ever, Malcolm

p.s. If Christianity was something we were making up, of course we could make it easier. But it is not. We cannot compete in simplicity with people who are inventing religions. How could we? We are dealing with fact. Of course anyone can be simple if he has no facts to bother about. C. S. Lewis

WHY ARE YOU A CHRISTIAN?

Dear Malcolm, You have excelled yourself telling me about the Trinity. I'm not sure I am any the wiser. You seem to be saying it doesn't really matter? Are you certain? Your reply is challenging, yet it has made me realise ancient church dogmas and creeds can, and should be debated.

We both know many atrocities have been carried out in the name of Christianity? What about other religions? Don't they reveal truth as well? Why have you chosen to be a Christian?

Hi Tom, you are absolutely right, there have been some very bad historical events carried out in the name of Christianity. The Crusades and the Spanish Inquisition are good examples. More recently, there have been clashes between Catholics and Protestants in Northern

Ireland. Violence tends to erupt when people feel they are right and everybody else is wrong. This happens especially when people feel certain God is on their side and their view is supported by God. Sadly, many people who claim to be religious carry out terror attacks to kill and maim innocent bystanders. However, evil deeds can be carried out by anyone whether or not they are religious. Lenin, Stalin, Hitler, Pol Pot, Saddam Hussein are just a few names I could mention who have carried out atrocities in order to demonstrate their power and eliminate all opposition. Religion is sometimes an excuse for people to carry out such deeds, but it is by no means the only excuse. Acting violently towards our fellow human beings is the exact opposite of what Jesus taught.

You ask why I am a Christian. I've mentioned in an earlier email that I was brought up in a Christian home. However, that did not make me a Christian. As someone once remarked, God has no stepsons. We have to discover our own beliefs and not simply mimic the religious convictions of our parents. We have to find God for ourselves because it is a personal relationship. This can be a struggle because sometimes we may disagree with our parents and loved ones. A major break for me was reading a book called 'Honest to God' by John Robinson who was a bishop in the Church of England. He presented a number of controversial, theological opinions I was already thinking about. If a bishop can think like this, I thought, I must be a Christian after all!

I knew a lady who cut off the end of the bone every time she had a joint of meat. When her partner asked why she did this she replied because her Mum had always done it. When she asked her Mum why she did it, she said because she never had a roasting tin big enough. We all have parental viewpoints which we have internalised and which influence us, but ultimately we have to determine the extent to which our parents have influenced our religious beliefs, and in so doing we find our own identity and, in the context of the Gospel, become followers of Jesus. This is at the heart of Jesus' teaching about leaving ones father and mother. (Luke 14: 26) It is our internal parents we have to deal with; those parental voices within us which are usually full of 'shoulds' and 'oughts'.

My Christian faith strengthened when I left home to train to be a teacher of mathematics and later, to read psychology at Goldsmiths College in London. I went through an agnostic phase but honestly there are many beliefs I am still agnostic about in my retirement. For example, I remain open to what exactly happened on the first Easter or how the Holy Spirit empowered the disciples or the precise time line of those events. Somebody once said to me, 'hold on to Jesus Christ and for the rest be totally uncommitted'. I thought this was very sound advice and it has stood me in good stead throughout my life.

Many people believe faith in Jesus is simply a crutch to lean on in times of trouble. I know a crutch can be an essential piece of equipment if we have a broken limb. A crutch offers much needed support and help but Jesus is much more than a crutch. For me Jesus is an inspiration. He spoke a lot about the Kingdom of God, a place where gospel teachings influence people's families and relationships. Wouldn't it be wonderful if people lived more loving lives and did to others what they wanted others to do to themselves. If, instead of despair, there was hope, instead of war, peace, instead of hate, love. Can you imagine a world like that? Isn't that inspiring and something to work towards? Surely love must be better than hate. What has hate ever achieved?

If you want to know about the values of the Kingdom of God then please read the Sermon on the Mount which you find in Matthew's gospel chapters 5, 6, and 7. There you will see how difficult the Christian life can be.

'If anyone strikes you on the right cheek, turn the other one also'.

'Love your enemies and pray for those who persecute you'.

'If someone forces you to go one mile, go also the second mile'.

'Do not swear at all'. Don't use the name of God as a curse'.

'Do not store up for yourselves treasures on earth, where moth and rust consume and where thieves break in and steal; but store up for yourselves treasures in heaven, where neither moth nor rust consumes and where thieves do not break in and steal. For where your treasure is, there your heart will be also.'

These are just a few verses from the Sermon on the Mount and you can see immediately how difficult they are to put into practice. G.K.Chesterton once said the Christian life hasn't been tried and found wanting, it has been tried and found too difficult. Never think being a Christian is easy. I have struggled with it all my life. If I look again, for example, at those verses from the Sermon on the Mount I ask myself how often have I fallen short, and that, sermon, is the heart of the gospel. I am far from complete as a Christian, more a work in progress. There is a subtle difference between being a Christian and being Christian. The latter, the adjective, implies the question, how Christ like am I? I can readily claim to be a Christian but how far am I following the demands of the gospel? Is my life always a life of love? Do I readily love my neighbour as myself? Do I always pray for those I dislike? Do I always go the extra mile? How easy is it for me to walk the way of the cross?

What I am certain of is the Christian faith has given me a foundation, an anchor on which to base my life. The anchor has enabled me to explore the mystery we call God. I am convinced there is far more to this world than what we can see. I am also convinced present day scientific knowledge doesn't have all the answers; it is constantly making new discoveries. Science has actually deepened my faith when I consider what a wonderful world we live in and how amazingly complex and yet finely tuned our bodies are.

Scientific research attempts to answer the 'how' questions whilst religion strives to answer the 'why' questions. The most important question is 'why are we here?' and we all have to find an answer to that question, an answer which satisfies and gives all of us a foundation stone to life.

Oh yes, you did ask about other religions. Well, for some people, Christianity is the only answer but I believe this viewpoint is very exclusive. We live in a multicultural society and to say Christianity is the only way to discovering the truth about life, thereby excluding any truth that other religions hold, seems very hard to justify. It doesn't make any sense to me to affirm God can only be known through one religious tradition. By chance, that just happens to be my own! Moreover, if God can only be known through Christianity this would imply we have to be a Christian in order to experience God. Where does that leave the central idea of the grace of God? Grace is a free gift of God and does not, therefore, need any prior requirement.

In my youth I used to climb mount Snowdon in North Wales. There are different ways to the summit depending on where you start from. I think there are different ways into the mystery of God and the mysteries of religions and life. Other religions also point the way to love and peace; they are the product of the culture and environment giving birth to them. If I had been born into another culture there is a high probability I would have been a Buddhist or Hindu or whatever.

I hope this letter finds you well and fulfilled in your life and work.

LOL, Malcolm

p.s. Go for what you believe in. Don't take no for an answer.

IS CHRISTIANITY PAST ITS SELL BY DATE?

Dear Malcolm, I'm wondering whether the church in the West has past its sell by date. Whenever I find myself in a church service the congregation is often small, and those in attendance seem elderly. I'm not against small congregations but if there are no young people I just wonder what the future holds for the Christian church in the U.K. Has the church past its sell by date?

Dear Tom, as a Methodist minister, I never wanted to be the curator of a museum, I looked forward to a vibrant and growing congregation. Unfortunately, in many villages, towns and cities church membership is continuing to decline because church services are unattractive especially to young people. Many long standing church members, for example, are reluctant to change the format or even the time of their Sunday services.

My wife, Lucy, often presents me with a good idea. When she does I go into a very defensive mode because I know for sure, even if it is a good idea, I will have to change my set routines in some way. I'm quite happy with the way I am thank you! Our minds just do not like change. They resist it every way they can.

Unfortunately, I have on occasions reached the conclusion church members enjoy controversy. Replacing Victorian wooden pews with comfortable chairs and changing the times of services during the winter months are often frowned upon. Changes can be resisted by church leaders and congregations alike, yet we know from industry the most important principle of successful management is 'change or die'. Many well-known High street stores have recently closed because they were unwilling to adapt their businesses to internet selling. Farmers, for example, have had to change their cultivation and harvesting techniques in order to keep up with the competition and demand. In nature, insects, and animals have adapted to changing environments through the course of natural selection and evolution.

The stubbornness of many congregations to adapt has led to, or is leading to, their decline and ultimate closure. In some instances, senior members have been unable to adopt the ideas of younger people or accept that they enjoy using electrical guitars and recorded music to accompany their singing. I love the church organ, but fully understand it is not the best musical instrument to encourage younger people to enjoy church music. There are many and varied ways in which we can worship.

There is a deeper reason why many people have drifted away from going to church. Some used to attend when they were young, but now only make an effort to go at Easter or for the Christingle service at Christmas, or not at all. The Christian church is partly to blame for decline in membership and attendance. For centuries it ruled people's lives and their daily behaviour, and treated hard working class labourers as illiterate peasants. The priesthood instilled fear of hell and eternal damnation, and insisted biblical stories could not be questioned. It blinkered rational thinking and intellectual curiosity as a means of its preservation, and shuddered when secular thinking questioned authority. Its recent downfall has been enhanced by sexual scandals amongst some clergy, and there is now the freedom to shop and play sport on Sundays.

In a strange sense people are now getting ' their own back' on centuries of church oppression. If those in authority had bothered to inform members of their congregation they were free to question ancient dogmas and creeds, attendance may not have fallen so rapidly. Sadly, they have ' lost the battle', most of the present generation of young people have little interest in church services, have a minimum knowledge of biblical stories, and would probably be offended if a priest or vicar questioned their absence from mass or communion.

It is realising the world we live in is so radically

different from that depicted in the bible. The world today is poles apart even from the world I grew up in. I think there is also a feeling that science can supply all the answers. A radical difference is globalisation, the world seems to have become very much smaller. This is largely as a result of instant communications and easy travel. There is also a mass movement of people, increasingly we live in a country alongside folk of other faiths, race, and cultures. Christianity, like other faiths, has the challenge of reimagining God, Jesus and the church in this multicultural environment. In our country the church is finding itself in exile. People no longer know what Pentecost is. Good Friday is just like any other day, and Sunday has become like any day of the week. We are no longer living in a Christian country. People are worshipping the gods of sport and consumerism. Christianity is simply not part of people's lives. If it is anywhere at all it is on the edge of life. It may be argued this is a good place to be rather than a place of cultural privilege, but from there it can lend a different viewpoint on society. Being on the edge of a situation leads to a more objective viewpoint than when one is fully immersed in a situation.

Interestingly, the church is growing in other parts of the world. In some African countries membership is increasing and in South Korea large numbers attend morning services. In China and Russia, after many years of oppression and persecution the church is beginning to grow. The church is certainly not dead yet. No doubt sociologists will come up with some reasons why this is the case. All I know for sure is the church in the West is in decline.

However, in England there are pockets of very vibrant and full churches which play an active part in the community. Messy Church encourages families into church to relax, play, worship and eat a meal. Other people are seeking out new ways of being church. My own conviction is there will always be people who want to worship, who want to gather round what we call the Lord's table, eat bread, drink wine, and remember Jesus' last supper. My guess is there will be fewer church buildings; many of them are very old and a drain on resources.

For the first three centuries of its existence the church actually grew without any buildings. The first Christians met in houses and it may well be that people start meeting in houses again and enjoying a meal together before joining in informal worship. This occurred in the 70s, 80s and 90s in what was called the house church movement and many people gained spiritual sustenance from it. Wherever churches are alive, they worship and live in a way that connects people with God and builds a loving, supportive community. In summary, I think the church will cease to exist in its present form in this country, but Christianity will most certainly continue in some shape or other.

I hope this series of emails has helped you with your questions Tom. There is no way I can convince you about the truth of Christianity any more than I can talk you into falling in love with someone. Such things are more affairs of the heart than the head. Of course, our heads are also important. I've used my head in replying to your questions! We need to use them also in matters of the heart. It is a question of balance. Churches have a tendency to concentrate on one or the other. Some congregations seem to leave their heads on the doorstep when they enter their church and believe everything without thinking. Other congregations leave their hearts on the church doorstep and participate in a very dry, cerebral form of worship.

Please keep asking questions. This is very important. Constantly exploring the mystery we call God continues to be a fascinating journey for me. My hope and prayer is that you discover a faith relevant to this day and age, and you will find a group of like-minded friends to offer love and support so you become the person God wants you to be.

Lots of love, Malcolm

ALL A DELUSION?

Dear Malcolm, I know you thought you had received my last email, but I'm afraid I have one more. I have just read Richard Dawkins book, 'the God Delusion'. He says that having a religious faith is very infantile and we might just as well believe in Santa Claus or the tooth fairy. In other words, belief is something we outgrow. He thinks violence in the world is caused by religion and, God is a delusion because there is no evidence. Belief in God is completely irrational. Dawkins says you might just as well believe a teapot is orbiting the sun. People seem to have a need and so God becomes a wish fulfilment. For Dawkins there are no limits to the scientific method; it is the only reliable way of understanding the world. In the course of time science will explain everything. As a scientist myself, I agree with his emphasis on the importance of empirical verification, but I wondered what you think. Are you deluded as well?

Dear Tom, I wasn't expecting to hear from you so soon. So you've been reading Dawkins!!! Many people are taken in by his forceful arguments, but I recommend you read a very good riposte to Dawkins. It's called 'The Dawkins Delusion' by Alister McGrath. All I can do here is make one or two points.

If belief in God and the value of religious belief are so infantile, notions we grow out of, why is it that some people convert to Christianity when they are older? A celebrated example is Professor Antony Flew, an English philosopher and outspoken atheist who stunned and dismayed the unbelieving faithful when he announced in 2004, at the age of 87, that God probably did exist. How many people believe in Santa Claus, or the tooth fairy in their older years?

Sadly, some violence in the world is caused by religion, but three noted atheists, Hitler, Stalin and Pol Pot, were responsible for a huge amount of horrendous evil in the last century. The reality of the situation is 'that human beings are capable of both violence and moral excellence – and that both these may be provoked by world views, whether religious or otherwise'. (McGrath p. 49)

Evidence for the existence of God was well researched at the beginning of the last century by William James in his classic, 'the varieties of religious experience' and more recently by people like David Hay. See, for example, his book entitled 'Exploring

Inner Space'. One also has to explain the amazing effect the life of Jesus has had on many millions through the centuries. The teachings of Jesus have been the foundation stone for the life of many people. There are many, many acts of kindness which have been carried out by people because of their Christian faith. To liken Christian principles and beliefs to flying teapots is beyond belief. McGrath writes, 'nobody I know believes such nonsense. But that's what Dawkins wants his readers to believe – that believing in God is on the same level as cosmic teapots'. (p.28)

For his ideas about wish fulfilment, Dawkins draws on the thoughts of the nineteenth century German philosopher, Feurbach, who also greatly influenced Sigmund Freud. Feurbach was an atheist who categorically asserted there is no God. People believe in God because they want to be consoled and comforted. Consequently, they project these longings or wishes, and call them God. God is simply the projection of human longings. McGrath asserts that 'wanting something is no demonstration that it does not exist.' (p.29) For example, we all need water and water certainly exists. Perhaps atheism itself is a response to human need, the desire for total independence. Is atheism itself a delusion?

As a scientist, Dawkins is on safer ground when he says that the only way of comprehending the world is through scientific method, he just cannot understand why any scientist should believe in God, yet many scientists do. McGrath himself, in his early life, was an atheist and studied molecular biophysics but gave up active scientific research to study theology. He quotes Gould, a scientist at Harvard. Though an atheist, Gould 'was absolutely clear that the natural sciences - including evolutionary theory- were consistent both with atheism and conventional religious belief.' (p.ix) 'Dawkins is forced to contend with the highly awkward fact that his view that the natural sciences are an intellectual superhighway to atheism is rejected by most scientists, irrespective of their religious views.' (p.20)

With regard to the limits of science, McGrath quotes Medawar, an Oxford immunologist and Nobel prize winner. Although a self-confessed rationalist Medawar says, 'that there is indeed a limit upon science is made very likely by the existence of questions that science cannot answer, and that no conceivable advance of science would empower it to answer…. I have in mind such questions as:

How did everything begin?

What are we all here for?

What is the point of living?' (p.18)

Scientific reasoning alone can neither refute, nor substantiate religious belief. Apart from scientific knowledge, there is intuitive knowledge and contemplative knowledge. Scientists love to talk about facts as though nothing else matters. They follow the example of Thomas Gradgrind in 'Hard Times' by Dickens. "In this life, we want nothing but Facts, Sir; nothing but Facts!" What about our feelings? Can these be classified as facts or empirically tested? I devoted a chapter to this in my earlier book 'Journeying with God'.

Dawkins expresses strong feelings when talking about God. One wonders where it is all coming from. At times he is so dogmatic and completely disregards evidence gathered over many centuries. McGrath quotes Eagleton, a literary critic:

'Such is Dawkins's unruffled scientific impartiality that in a book of almost four hundred pages, he can scarcely bring himself to concede that a single human benefit has flowed from religious faith.' (p.62) This is patently not true and really does not need me to give evidence to refute it.

Eagleton is known for his famous put down of Dawkins which again is quoted by McGrath 'Imagine someone holding forth on biology whose only knowledge of the subject is 'The Book of British Birds,' and you have a rough idea of what it feels like to read Richard Dawkins on theology.'(p.4)

Dear Tom, you asked whether I was deluded. I think Dawkins is more deluded than I am. He seems to have little understanding of theology, or faith or the bible. McGrath eloquently refutes Dawkins's rhetoric. I can only apologise for quoting McGrath at length. My suggestion would be that you buy the book for yourself.

As ever, lots of love, and, don't forget, keep asking questions! Malcolm

By the same author

Journeying with God, Epworth 2001

Sense and Nonsense, conversations with a clown about spiritual things, Author House 2011

Running the race, finding God in the London Marathon, Austin Macauley 2016

Behind enemy lines, Xlibris 2019